Drawing Music

The Tanglewood Sketchbooks

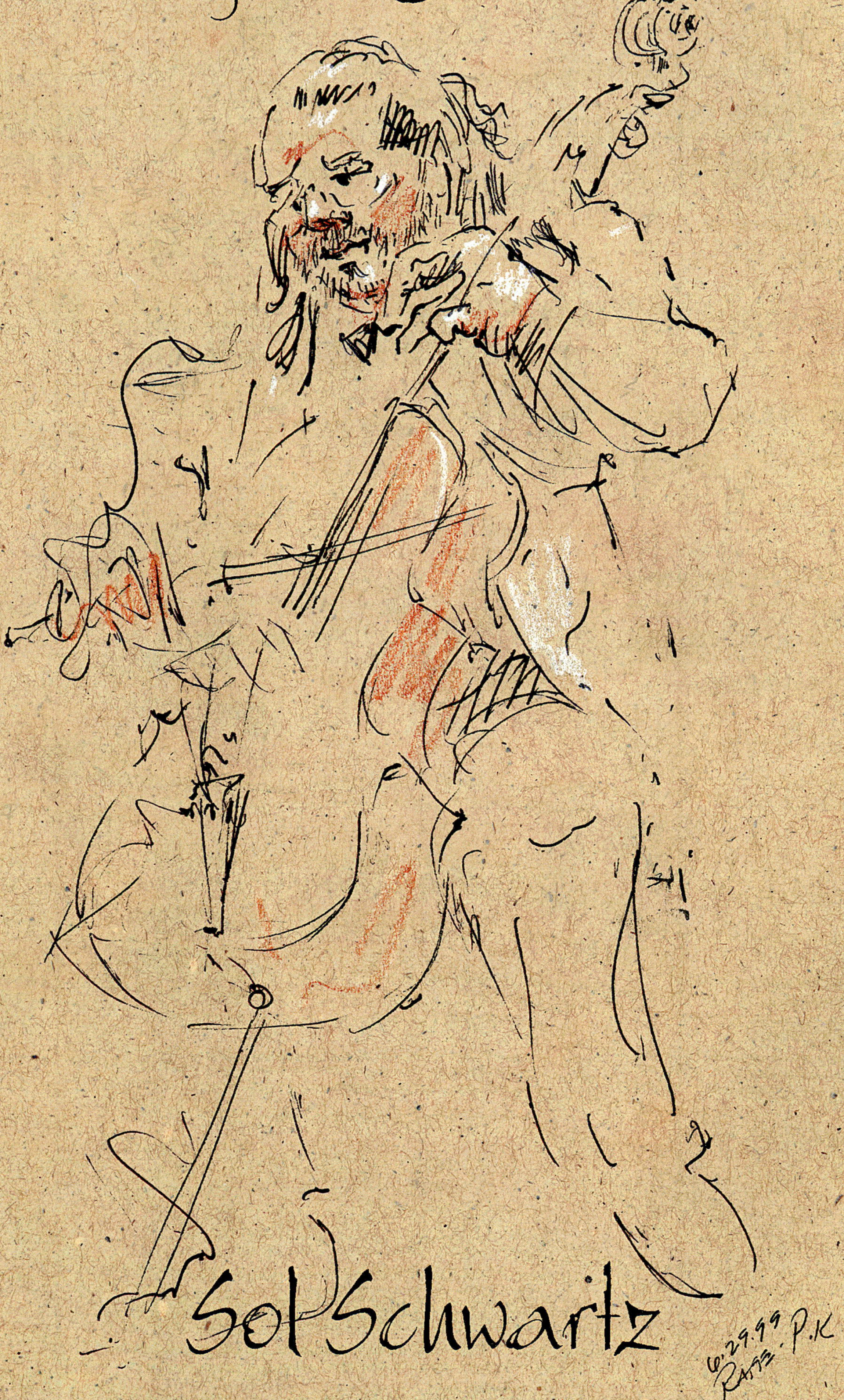

Sol Schwartz

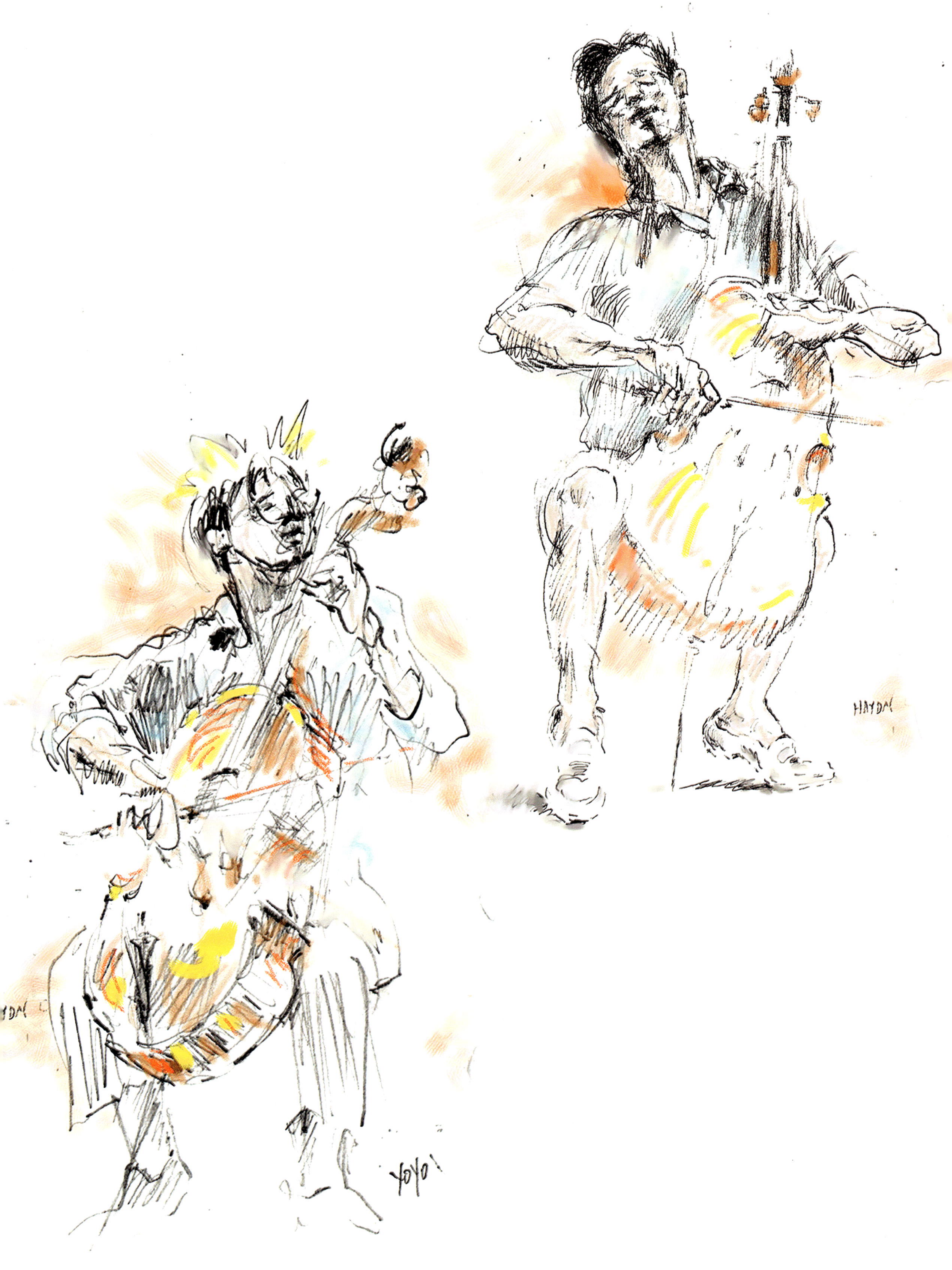
HAYDN
YOYO

This book is dedicated to the memory of
Lillian Linder Schwartz,
the light of my life.

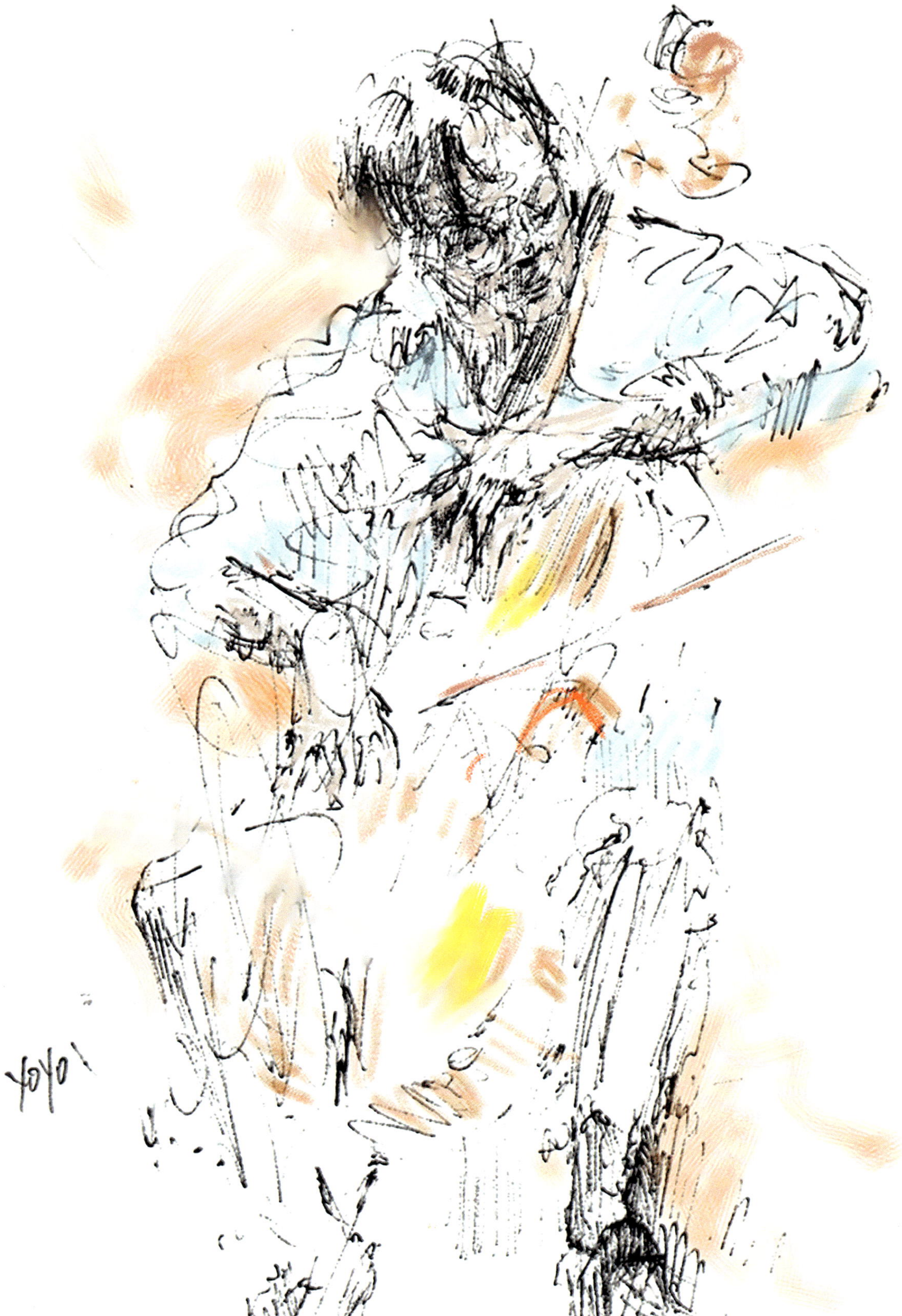

Drawing Music

FIRST EDITION

PRINTED IN THE USA, MAY 2001

ISBN NO. 0-9711342-0-0

PRINTED BY EXCELSIOR PRINTING COMPANY
60 ROBERTS DRIVE
NORTH ADAMS, MASSACHUSETTS 01247
413.663.3771

DIGITAL COMPILATION & DESIGN BY
TOM CROSS INC.
941.966.3843
607.692.4636

Many of the images in this book are available as limited edition fine art prints. For information, to contact the author, for art show schedules or for book ordering information contact:

Sol Schwartz Productions, Inc.
40 Frothingham Crossing
Lenox, MA 01240
413.637.2064

Cover notes of The Miles Davis recording, *Kind of Blue* entitled "Improvisation in Jazz", by Bill Evans, courtesy of Columbia Records.

Sol Schwartz divides his time playing the cello and drawing music in Lenox, MA and Sarasota, FL.

I want to thank the many friends and family members who have helped and encouraged me on this new venture.

I am grateful to you for helping make this book a reality.

Introduction

Live musical performance is ephemeral. It often feels as ephemeral as life itself. As a performer, one gives all one can give on the stage and then hopes that it was received and "heard" by the listener. And then it's over. When the performance "works", it may linger briefly in the air, but soon, a fine performance becomes a fond, but distant memory. This momentary quality is, indeed, part of what recommends live performance to us so powerfully. A live performance is the only true measure of what an artist can achieve and a recording of that performance is its aural document, a document of an artist's best impulses and fallibilities.

In his drawings of musicians, Sol Schwartz has achieved something amazing and marvelous of his own: he has over and over again described the moments of intense concentration, of communication, of effort and of unselfconsciousness that we, as performers, experience. In doing so, he has created another unique and wonderful document of our work: a visual one.

Great energy, the energy of music itself, suffuses Mr. Schwartz's drawings. One can see on his pages the complex process that is musical performance itself: the concentration on the music at hand, the artist's connection with the musical instrument, the electricity of just being on the stage, the communication between performers. But finally and above all, Mr. Schwartz has captured the unique stage and musical personality of each performer. And the sound of music permeates the atmosphere of each portrait. In his works, Sol Schwartz has generously documented those special moments, when humans made super-human efforts to communicate beauty to each other aurally.

As performers, we as artists are ever grateful that Sol Schwartz has helped our expression linger in the air yet a moment longer. We celebrate him for his work and for his musicality.

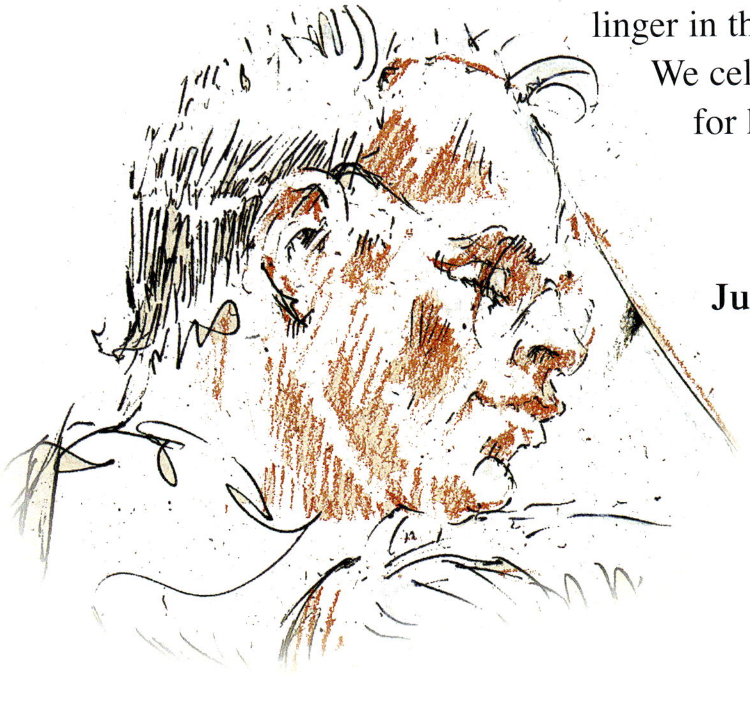

Joel Smirnoff
Juilliard String Quartet

"There is a Japanese visual art in which the artist is forced to be spontaneous. He must paint on a thin stretched parchment with a special brush and a black water paint in such a way that an unatural or interrupted stroke will destroy the line or break through the parchment. Erasures or changes are impossible. These artists must practice a particular discipline, that of allowing the idea to express itself in communication with their hands in such a direct way that deliberation cannot interfere.

The resulting pictures lack the complex composition and textures of ordinary painting, but it is said that those who see well find something captured that escapes explanation."

IMPROVISATION IN JAZZ
Bill Evans

(From the cover notes of the Miles Davis classic, Kind of Blue)

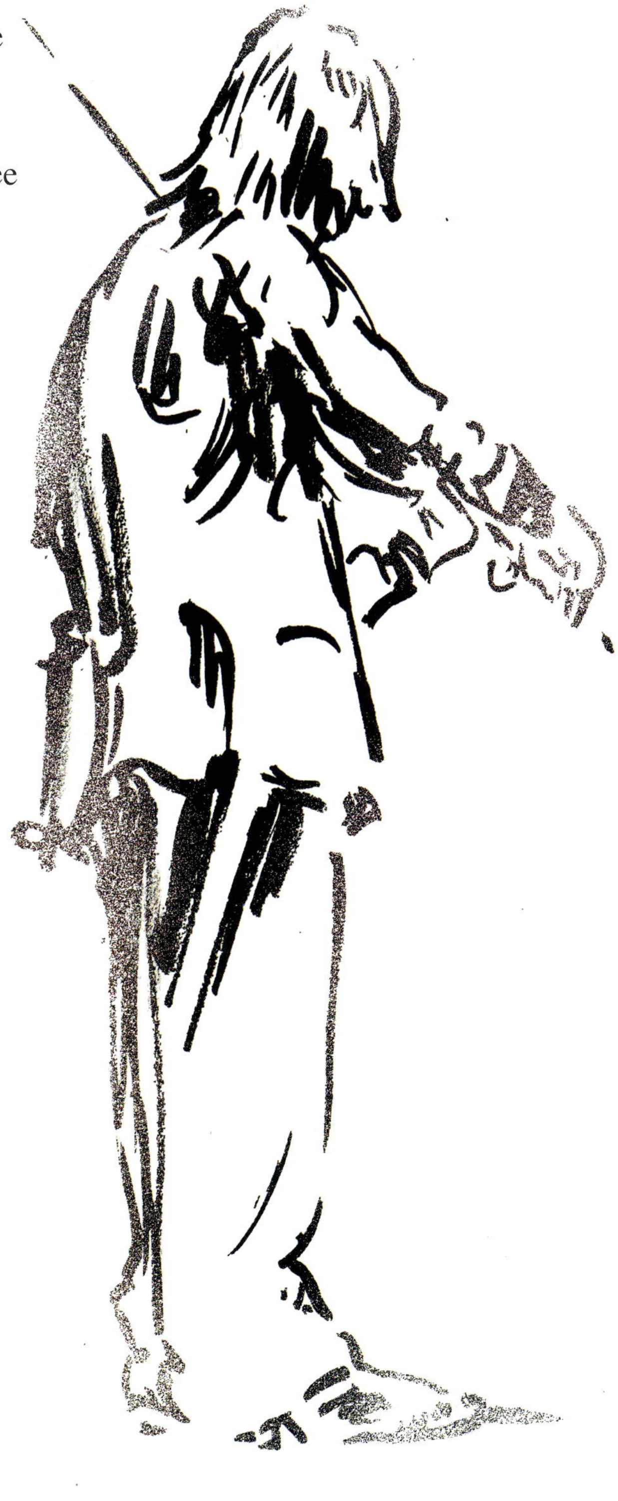

Prelude

Music and art return to my happiest educational years, as a fellow art student of Sol Schwartz, at Manhattan's public High School of Music and Art. Now known as Fiorello LaGuardia High, it has merged with Performing Arts, of Fame fame. Sound and sight belong together, above all in our youth, when what we see and hear is fresh, not afresh. Equally dedicated, students and instruction and creation seldom felt. Much the same climate pertains at Tanglewood, where Sol could continue the giving and taking experience between sound and line so significant to his early years. The rustic musical world, if in costly, privileged fashion, perpetuates the learning and sharing that made our adolescence a relatively bearable experience, one where common interests obliterated many barriers of and to self.

Auden wrote about the "beauty of the eye on the object look." A very different appeal is present in the musical eye. Inner directed, this is the vision of insight, one that awaits and creates the coming of a miraculous agency, expecting the right sound by an elusive combination of the mechanical, the technical, the inspirational, and by sheer good fortune. In ancient and medieval times music played a key role in linking earth and heaven, harmony tying this world to the next. Singers and instrumentalists still feel this, even if unaware of such exalted status. In our society we are even creating museums to the musical muses, deservedly to those that make music popular - with the movies, our major cultural achievement...

Sol's lyrical lines pay homage to the musician as chosen person, retracing the mysterious union of individual, instrument and passion - the glorious sense first experienced at Music & Art.

Notebooks in every sense, these pages, in their unassuming, effectively sketchpad like presentation, let us share the collective joy of hearing and seeing music made, we the beneficiaries of his arresting lines in all their ecstatic freedom and harmony.

Colin Eisler

Colin Eisler is the Robert Lehman Professor of Art History at New York University Institute of Fine Arts. He is regarded as a world authority on the art of drawing.

Drawing Music

I've been listening to music all my life and somehow I found myself drawing while listening. Perhaps it was the intangible part of music, so fleeting and dominated by time that lead me to try to preserve the moment through the permanence of a drawing.

I notice sometimes, stepping back from myself as I draw, that my hand stops at those pauses in the music where a drawing pencil or pen might be a disruption to another listener, and speeds up or slows down according to the rhythm and motion of the music. Sometimes the line is very light and dancing. Sometimes very heavy and plodding. This is what I mean by drawing music.

These drawings have been my private record of my experience with the different artists and chamber groups that I've heard. I never intended them for public viewing.

Sol Schwartz

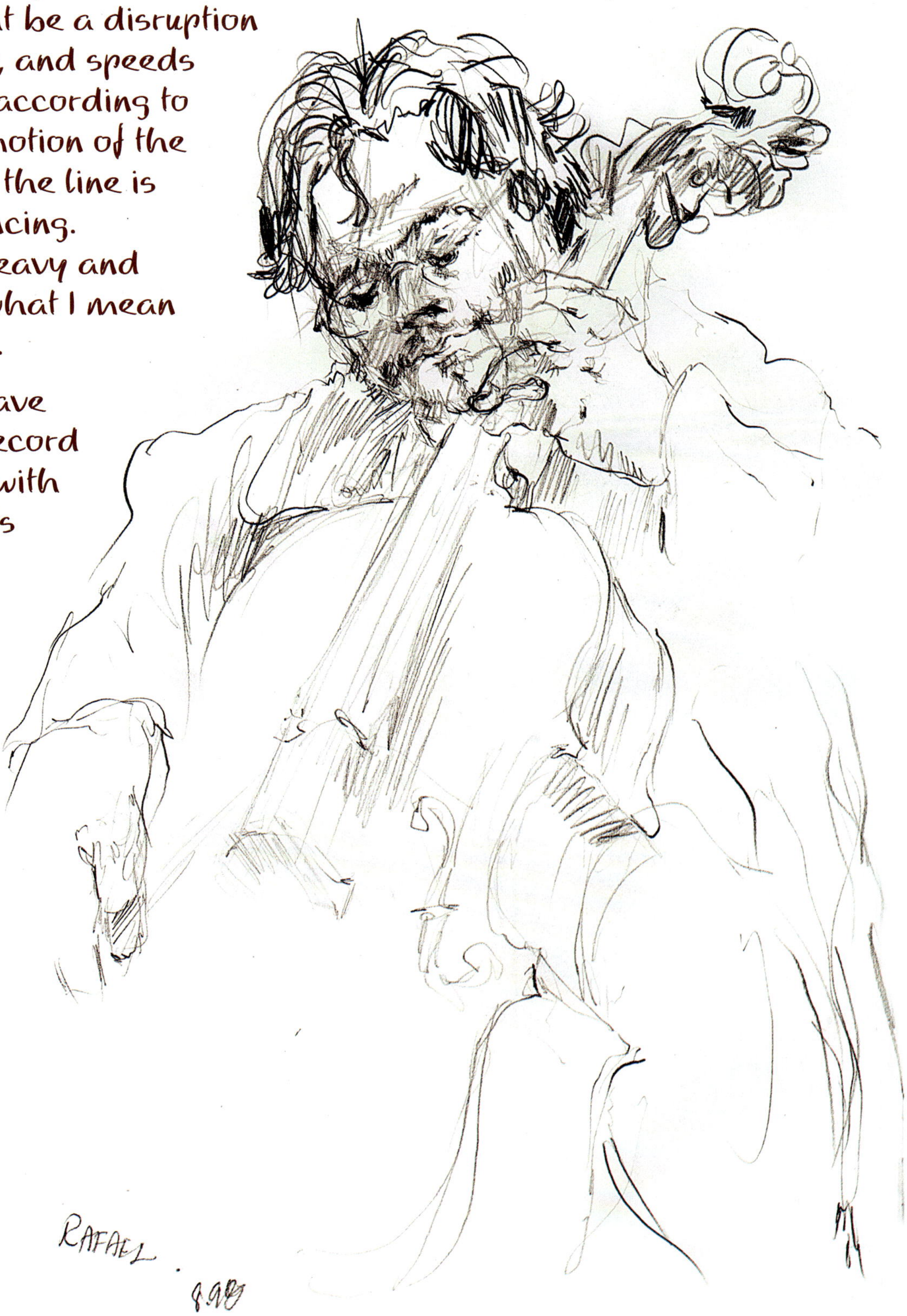

This is how it all began.

I was working as a volunteer in the Koussevitsky house, now the headquarters of the Tanglewood Visitors Center, a building that is not only used for visitors but for rehearsals and master classes.

A Tanglewood Music Center Fellow (student), Heath Marlowe was waiting for Joel Krosnick, his cello teacher. I drew the waiting student.

Joel Smirnoff, first violinist of the Juilliard String Quartet, walked in and looked over my shoulder. He said, "That looks just like him."

I asked, "Would you like to see your picture?" I turned the pages in my sketchbook to the drawing I had done a week earlier of the Juilliard in a recital at Ozawa Hall.

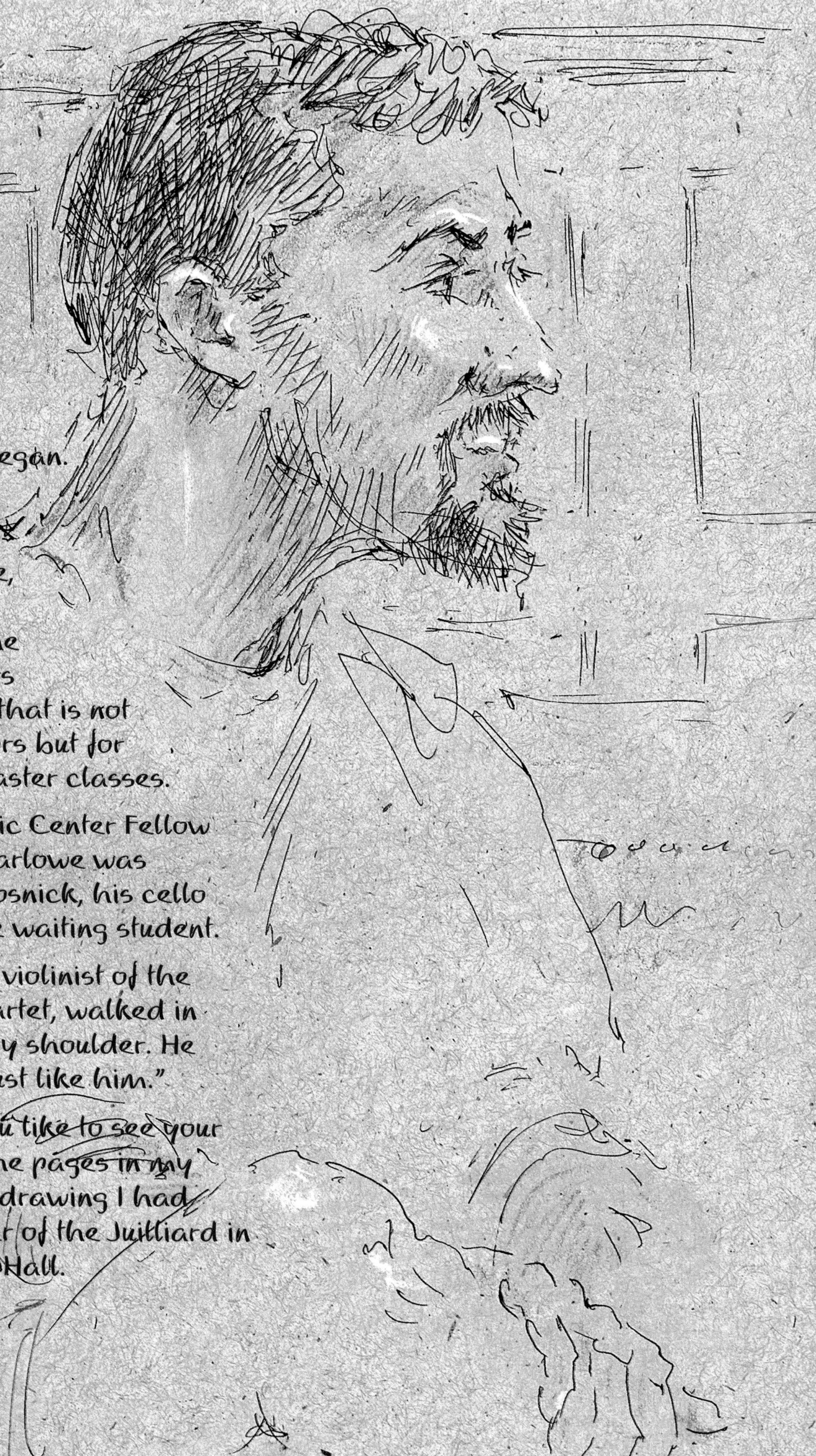

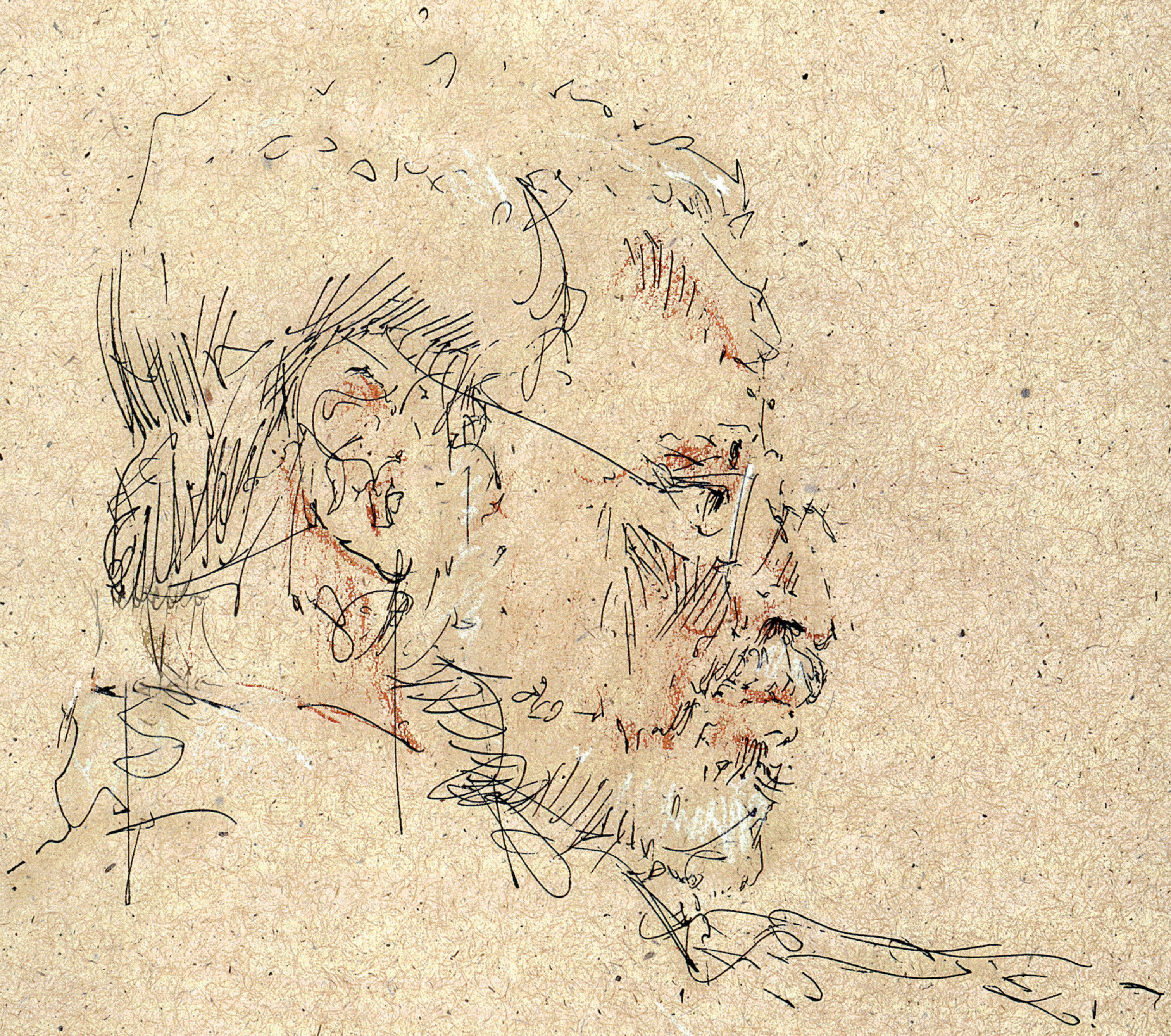

"Wow! That looks just like me," he said. "Do you have any others?"

I flipped back a few pages to show the others.

"I'll be right back with the quartet," he said.

In a few minutes the entire quartet was there. They looked over the drawings, then walked out to deliberate. Joel came back and said, "We took a vote. We'd like the drawings for our next CD."

JULLIARD QT.
6·27·99

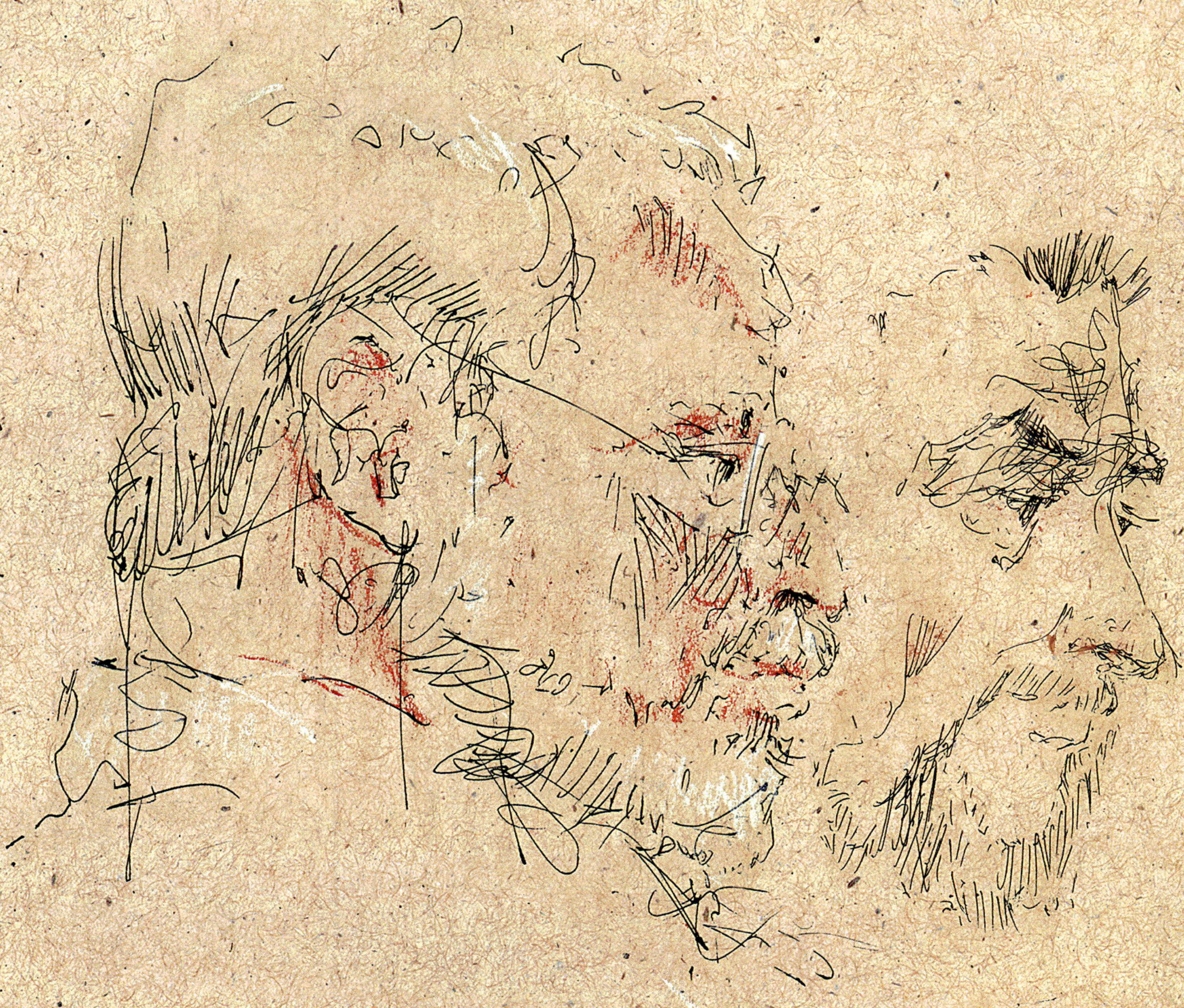

The Juilliard String Quartet

The Juilliard String Quartet, Joel Smirnoff (first violin), Ronald Cope (second violin), Joel Krosnick (cello) and Samuel Rhodes (viola) in performance at Ozawa Hall in Tanglewood.

JULLIARD QT.
6.27.99

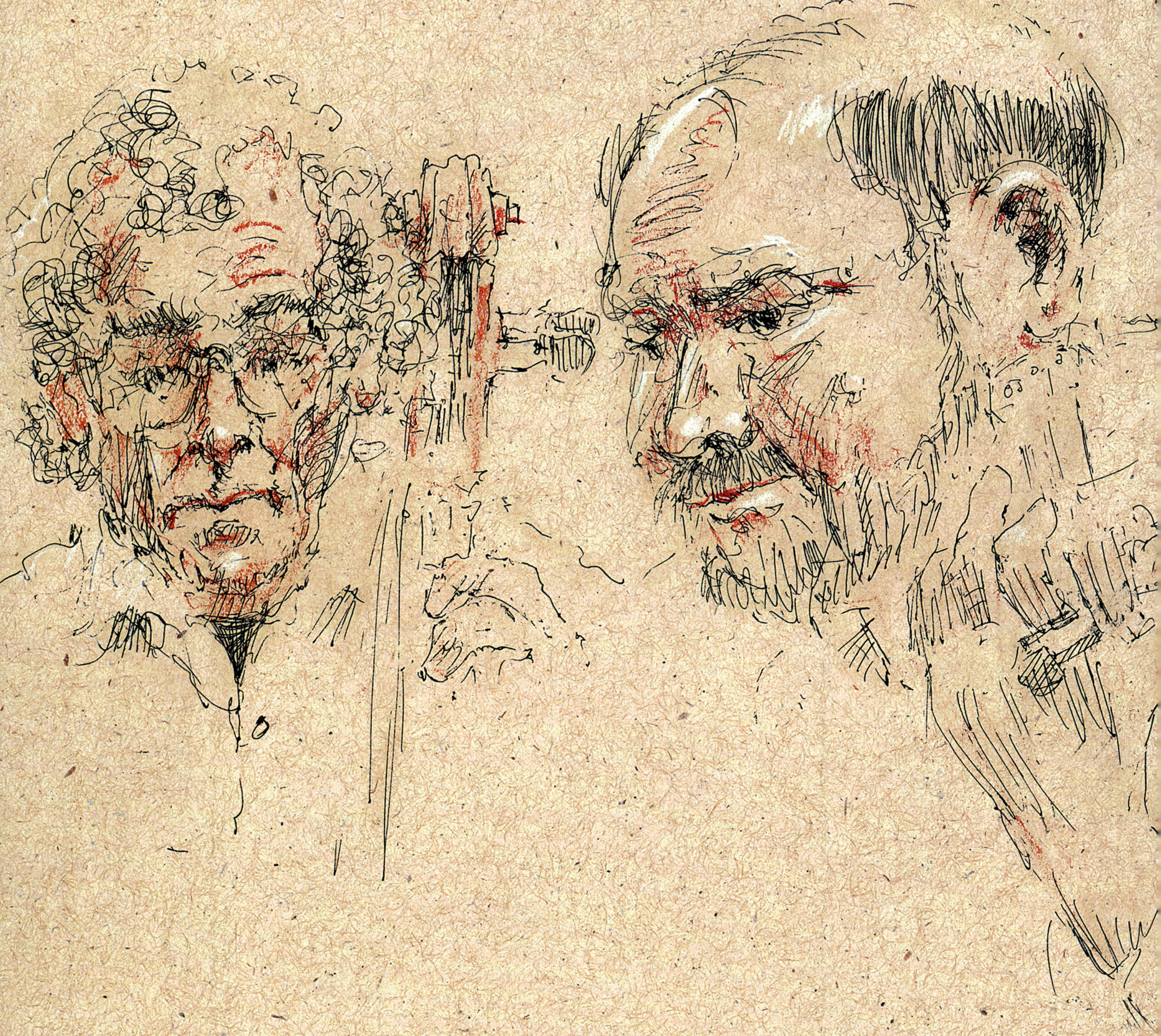

Joel Smirnoff saw me a few days later to pick up the drawings to take them to Sony. I said that I noticed that he had shaved off his beard. He looked about 20 years younger. "How are you going to put that drawing on the CD when you shaved it off?" I asked.

"Oh," he says, "by the time the CD comes out the beard will be back on."

He was coaching young and gifted artists from all over the world at the TMC. For the summer, the Julliard String Quartet is in residence to coach and perform as well. On Sundays the students perform and on this Sunday one of the quartets was scratched from the program because the first violinist was ill. A few minutes later someone came up to announce that Mr. Smirnoff was going home to get his violin. The quartet would play and he would join them. When he came on stage he went to the microphone and said, " I want you to know that I was never honored to be chosen a Tanglewood Music fellow and this is my debut doing the Eine Kleine Nacht music." This is a drawing of Joel, without the beard, playing with his eyes shut. It was an absolutely beautiful and memorable performance. I was very happy with the results because it caught the moment and the lightness and agility of his wonderful, wonderful playing. The student quartet may have been taken by surprise at the pace with which he took the music but nevertheless they stayed with him.

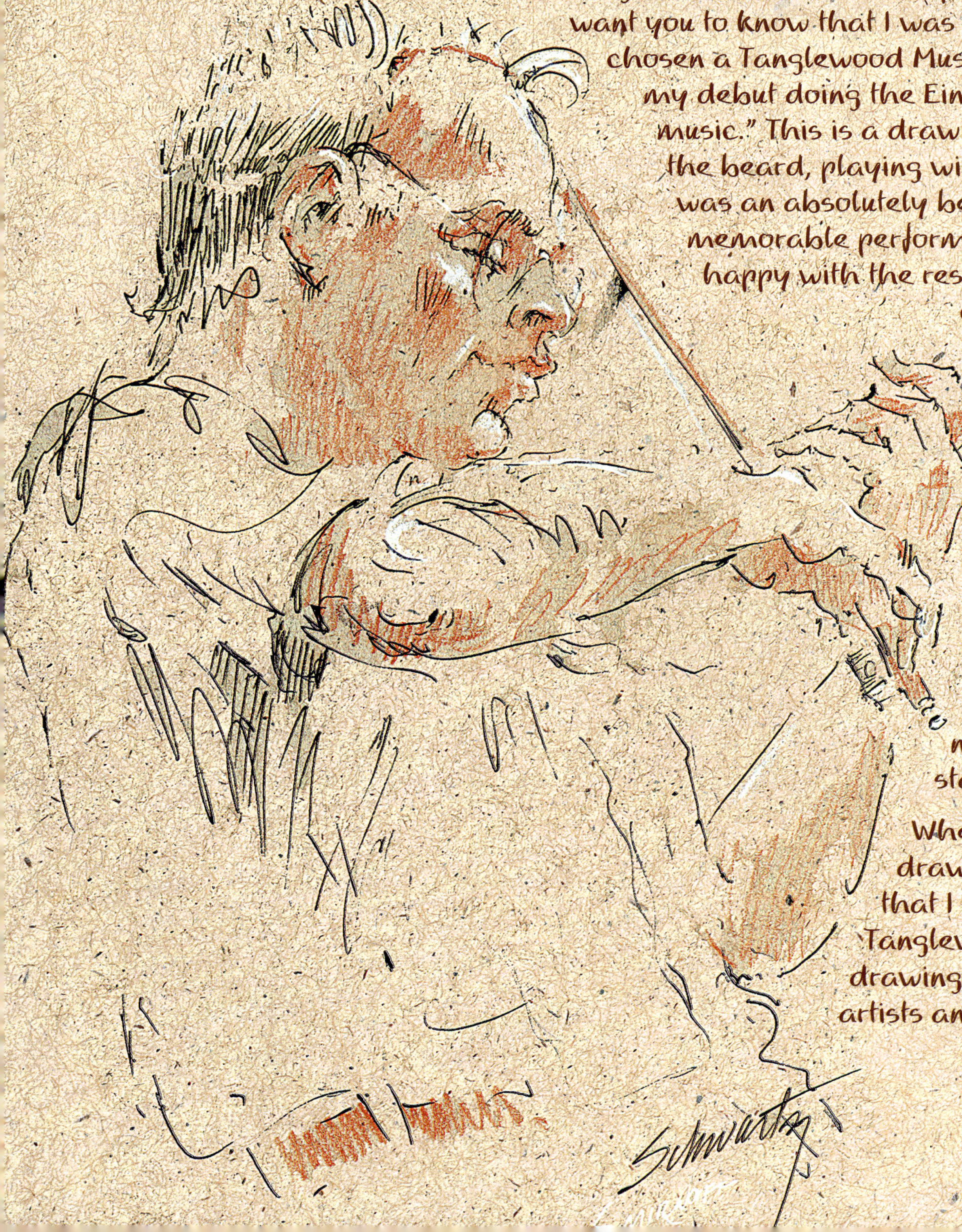

When he saw the drawing, Joel suggested that I do a book on Tanglewood using my drawings of conductors, artists and students.

This is a rehearsal of the TMC students, Ozawa is conducting and Joel Smirnoff sits on the podium making notes in the music on Ozawa's directions and passes on the directions to the students. The Gustave Mahler Youth Orchestra joined the TMC for this rehearsal.

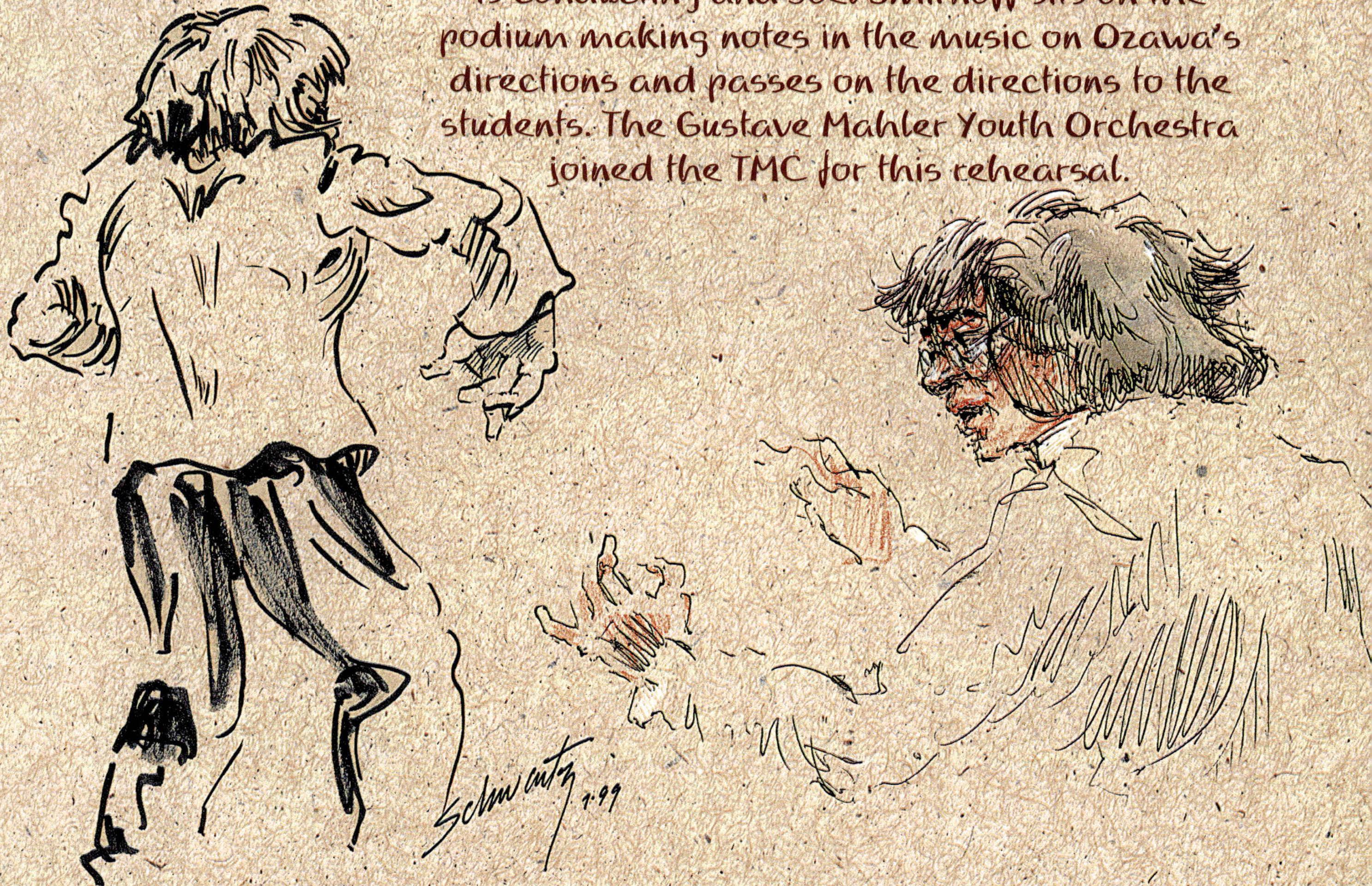

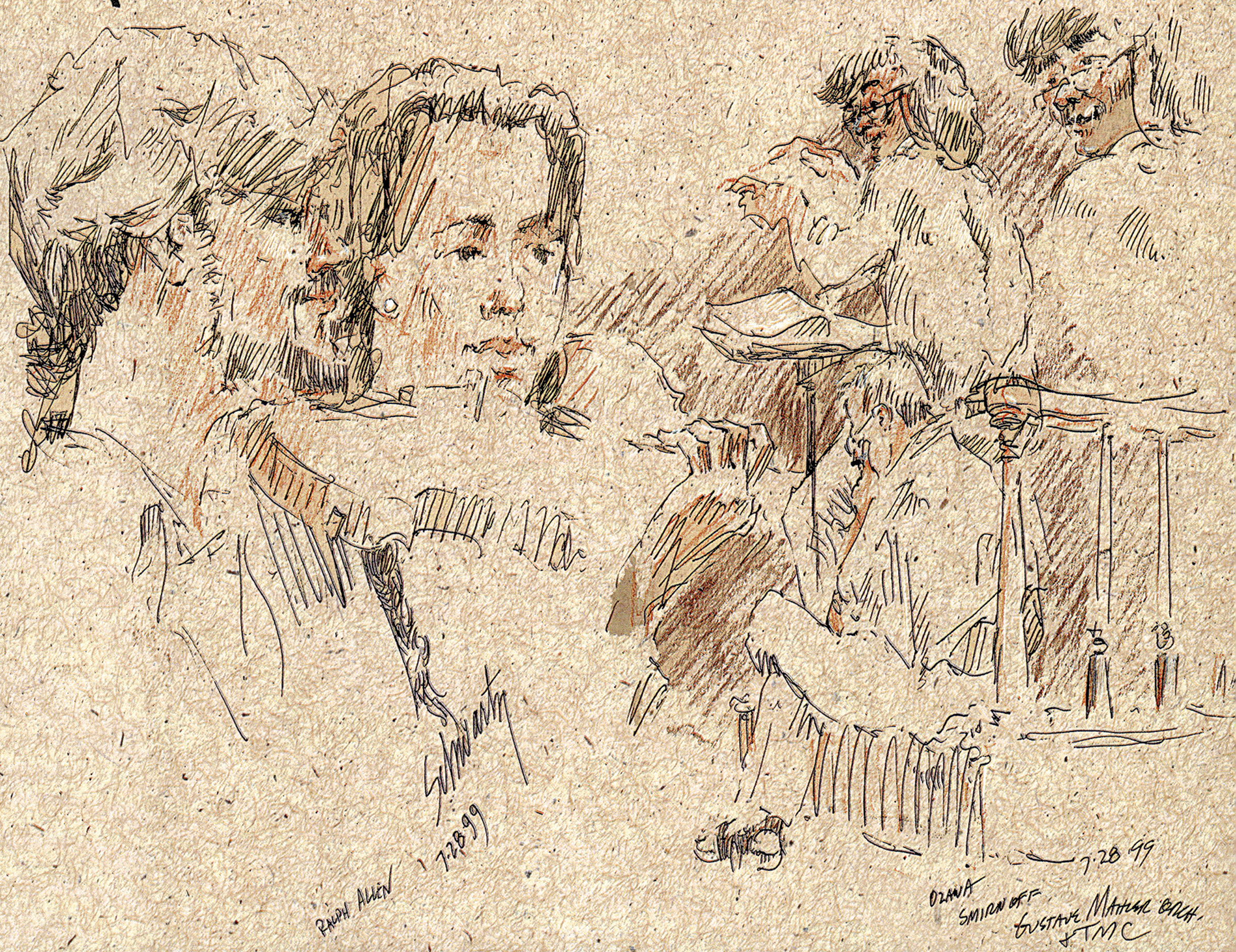

The Boston University Tanglewood Institute (Butis)

These talented high school-age students are the junior division of the Tanglewood music experience.

Here a group gathered at the end of the day in a practice studio to listen to a little Bach.

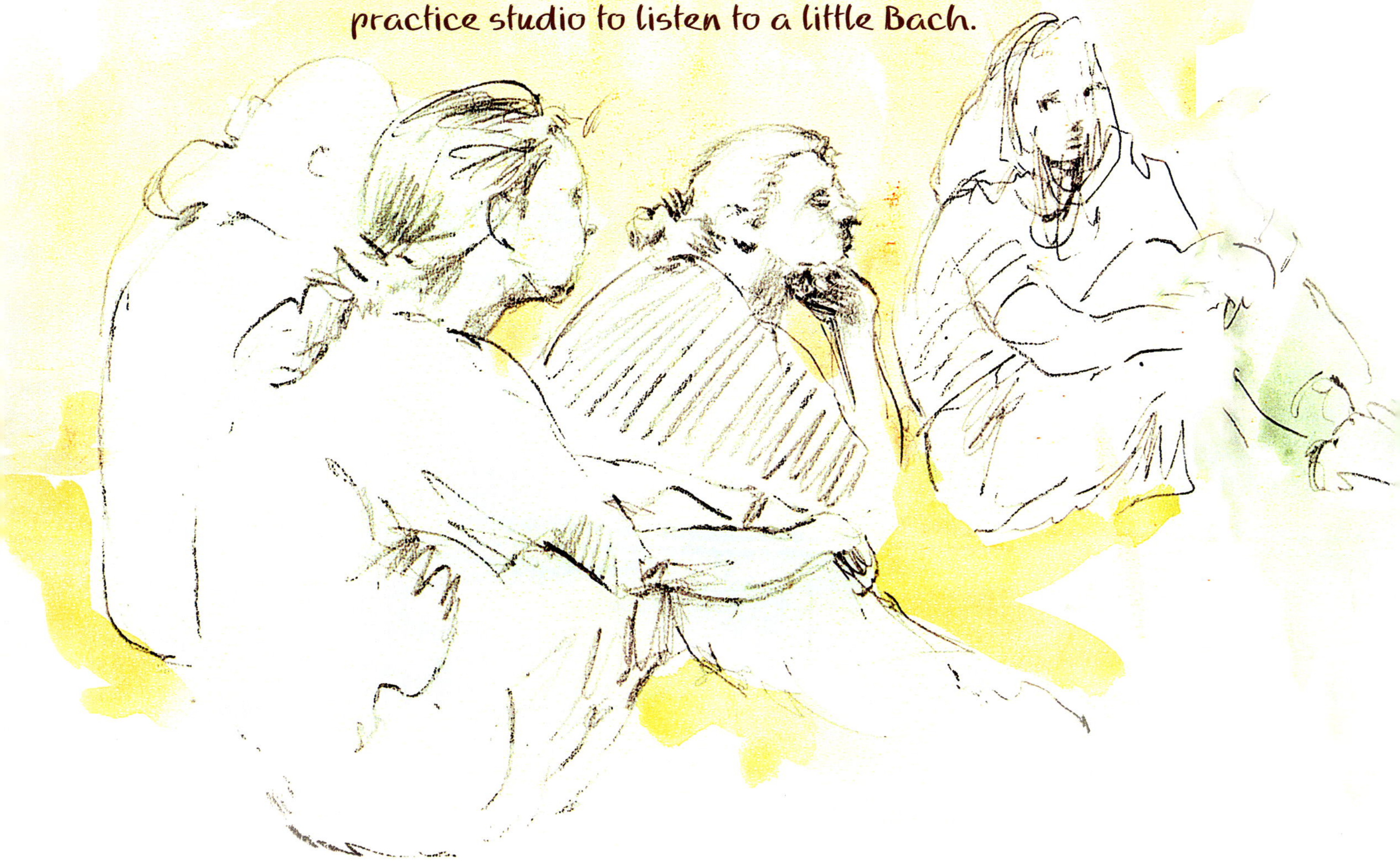

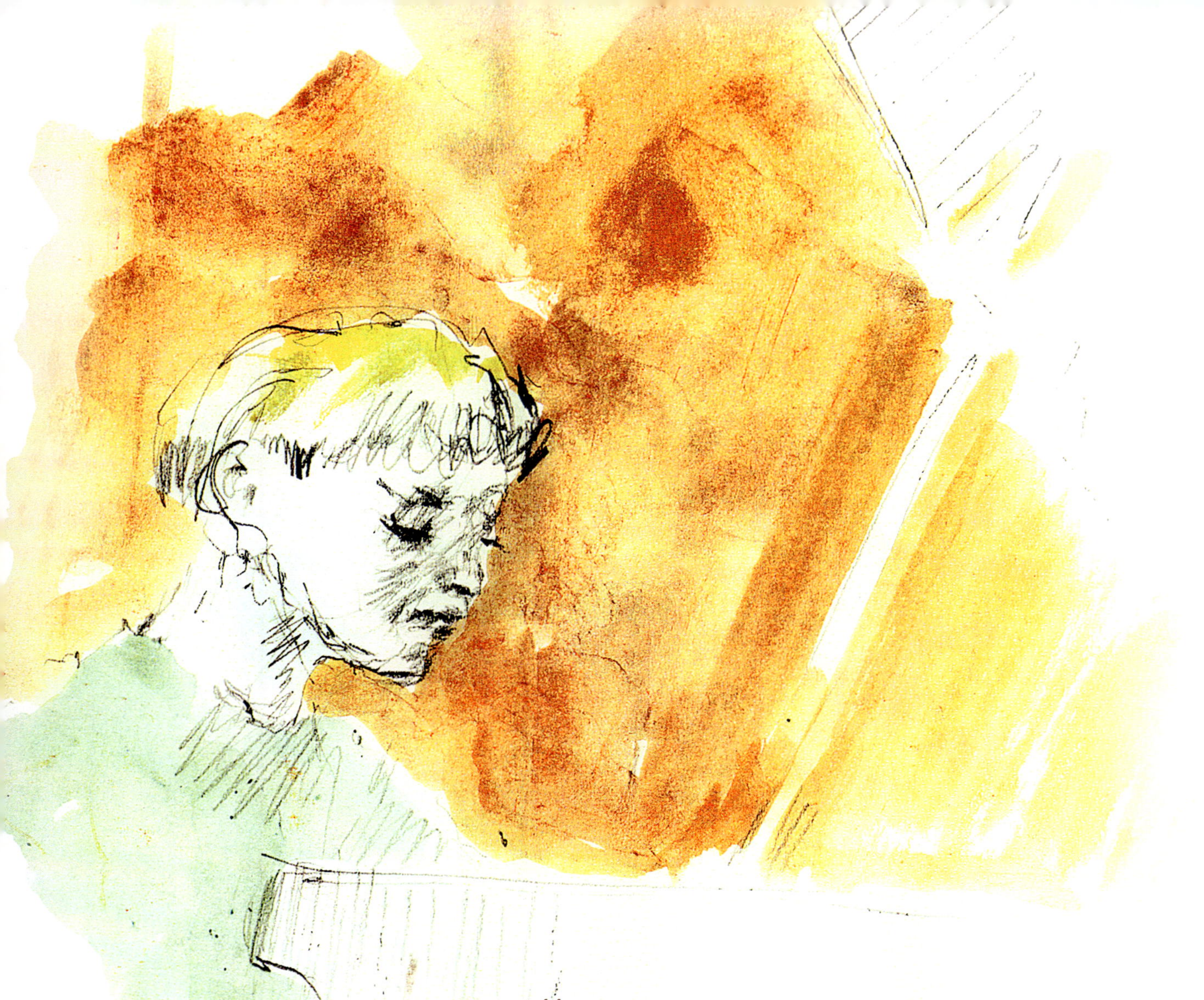

Joel Smirnoff was very encouraging about my creating a book. I agreed it might be a nice idea to release some of these drawings from the many notebooks I had been collecting. No one had ever seen* these sketches of Tanglewood soloists, conductors, and Boston Symphony members .

He especially requested images of the Tanglewood Music Center ("TMC") fellows, and the Boston University Tanglewood Institute ("BUTI") students that come here every summer.

We all come to this most exciting place, Tanglewood; where music is like the air you breathe, to be refreshed and exhilarated.

My sketchbooks are my attempt to capture these moments. That's how this book came to be.

* Except for the people who sit next to or in back of me.

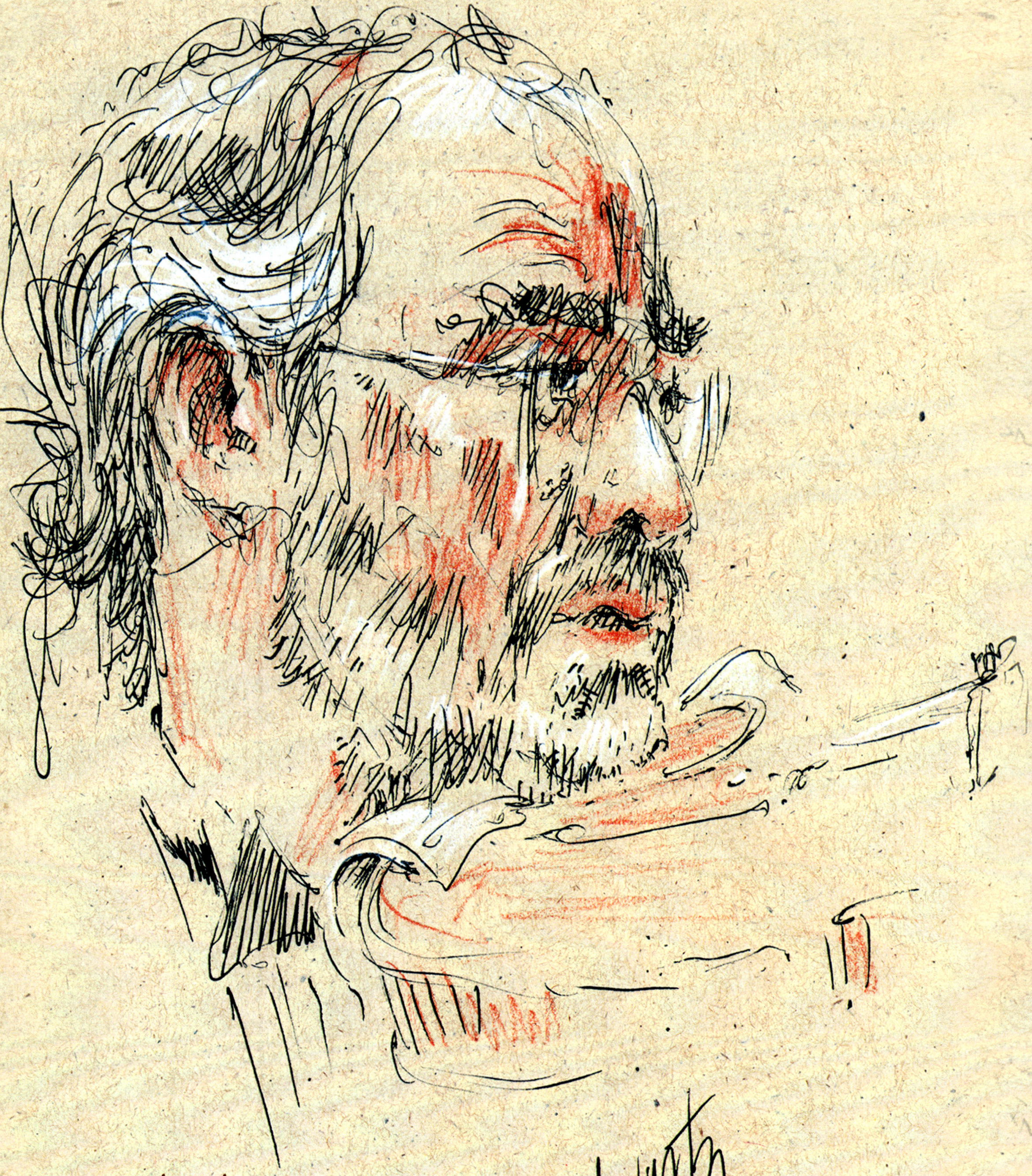

Malcolm Lowe

Malcolm Lowe is the concertmaster of the Boston Symphony Orchestra.

Emanuel Ax

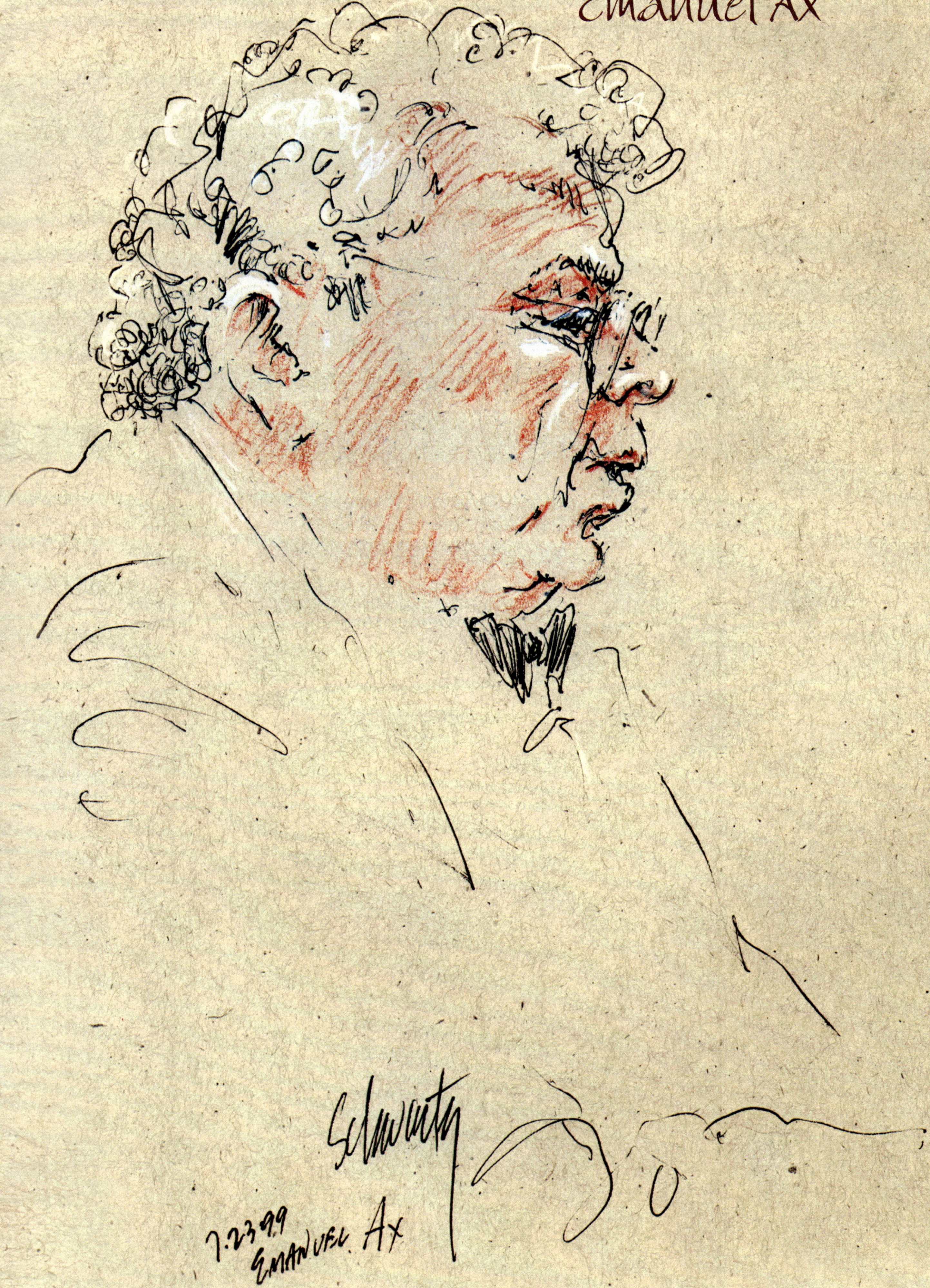

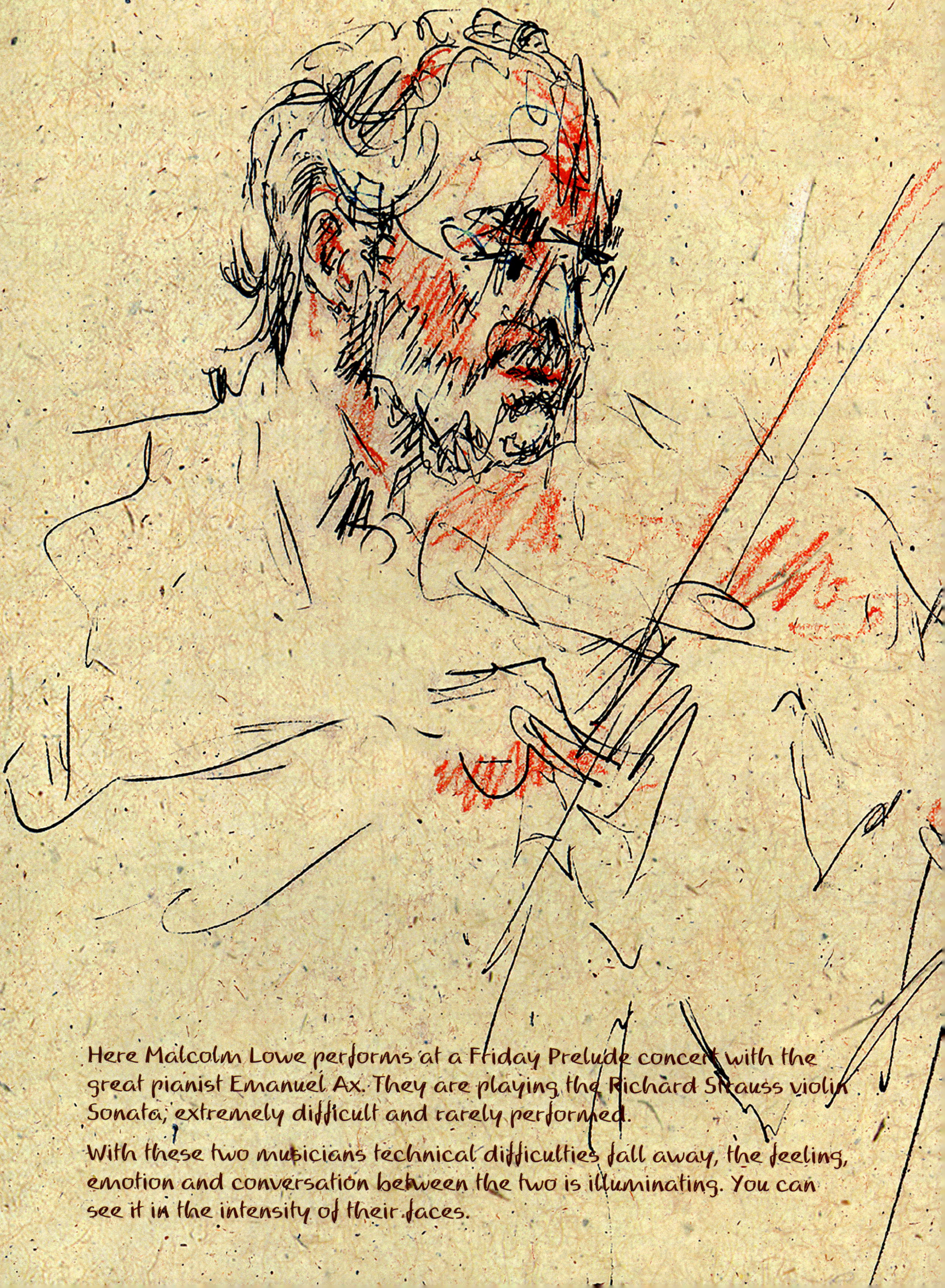

Here Malcolm Lowe performs at a Friday Prelude concert with the great pianist Emanuel Ax. They are playing the Richard Strauss violin Sonata, extremely difficult and rarely performed.

With these two musicians technical difficulties fall away, the feeling, emotion and conversation between the two is illuminating. You can see it in the intensity of their faces.

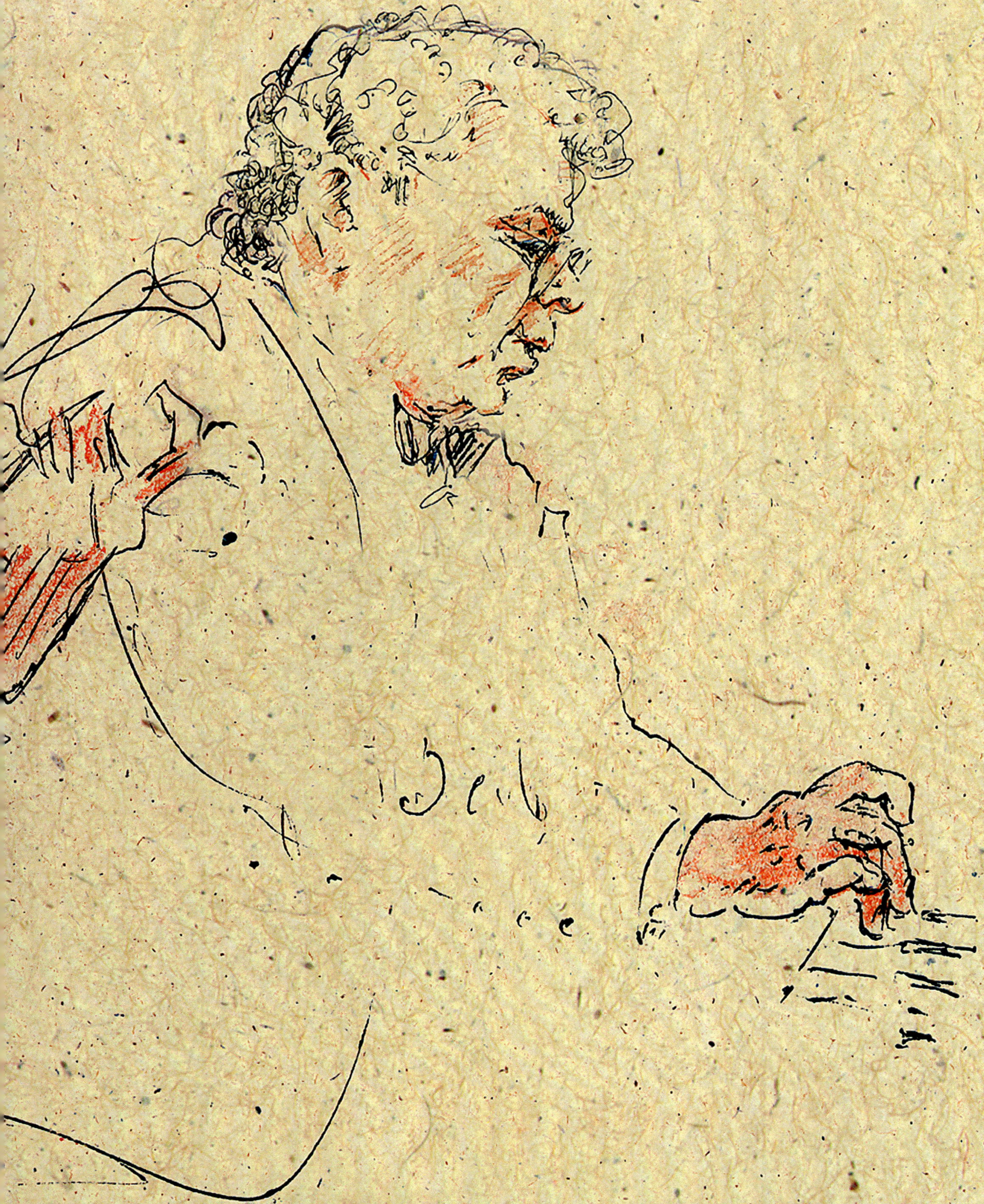

Mstislav Rostropovich

The Master Class

Mstislav Rostropovich came to Tanglewood at the end of last season to do a master class with the Tanglewood fellows. It was a closed session. I was permitted to come in because I had lent one of the students, Rafael Popper-Keizer, the music for the Ernest Bloch Shelomo, and Rafael had invited me. I drew the whole master class. It is the only visual record.

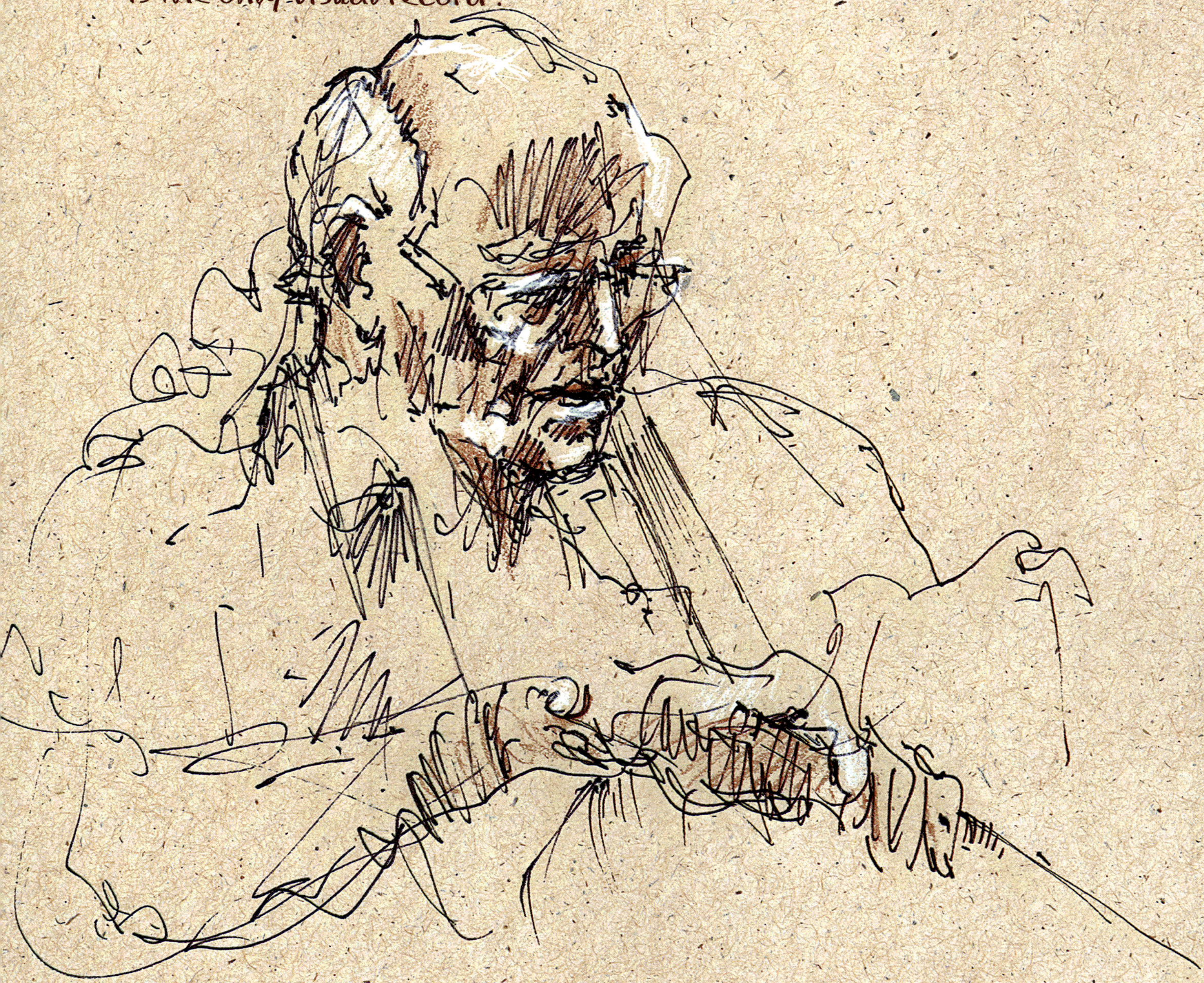

ROSTROPOVICH — SHOSTAKOVICH CONCERTO 8.98

In addition to the Master Class, Rostropovich performed two concertos and conducted Beethoven's Ninth Symphony with the BSO.

On the left he is rehearsing the Shostakovich cello concerto and below he is rehearsing for the Haydn cello concerto.

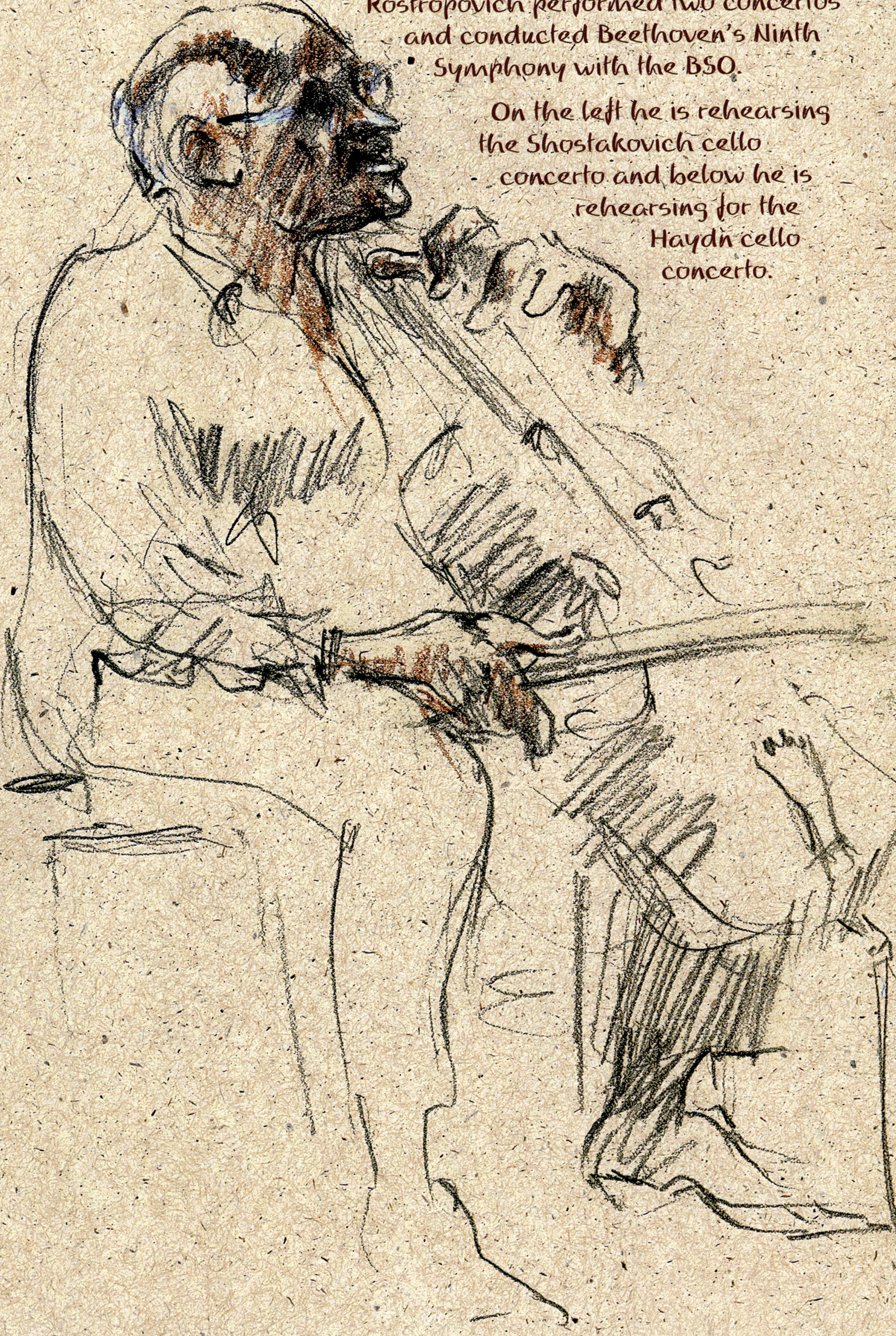

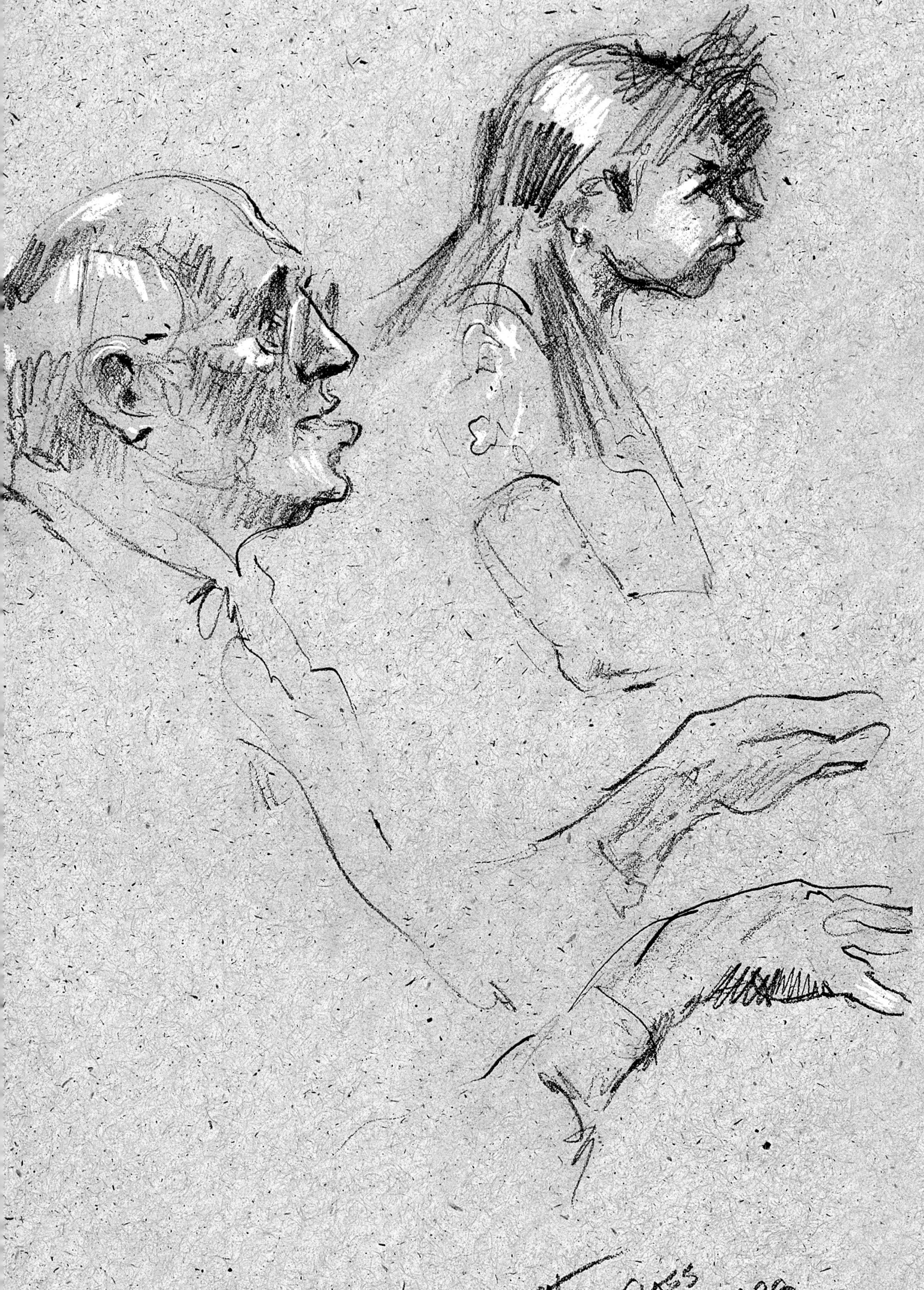
MASTER CLASS
8.25.98
HOSAKI

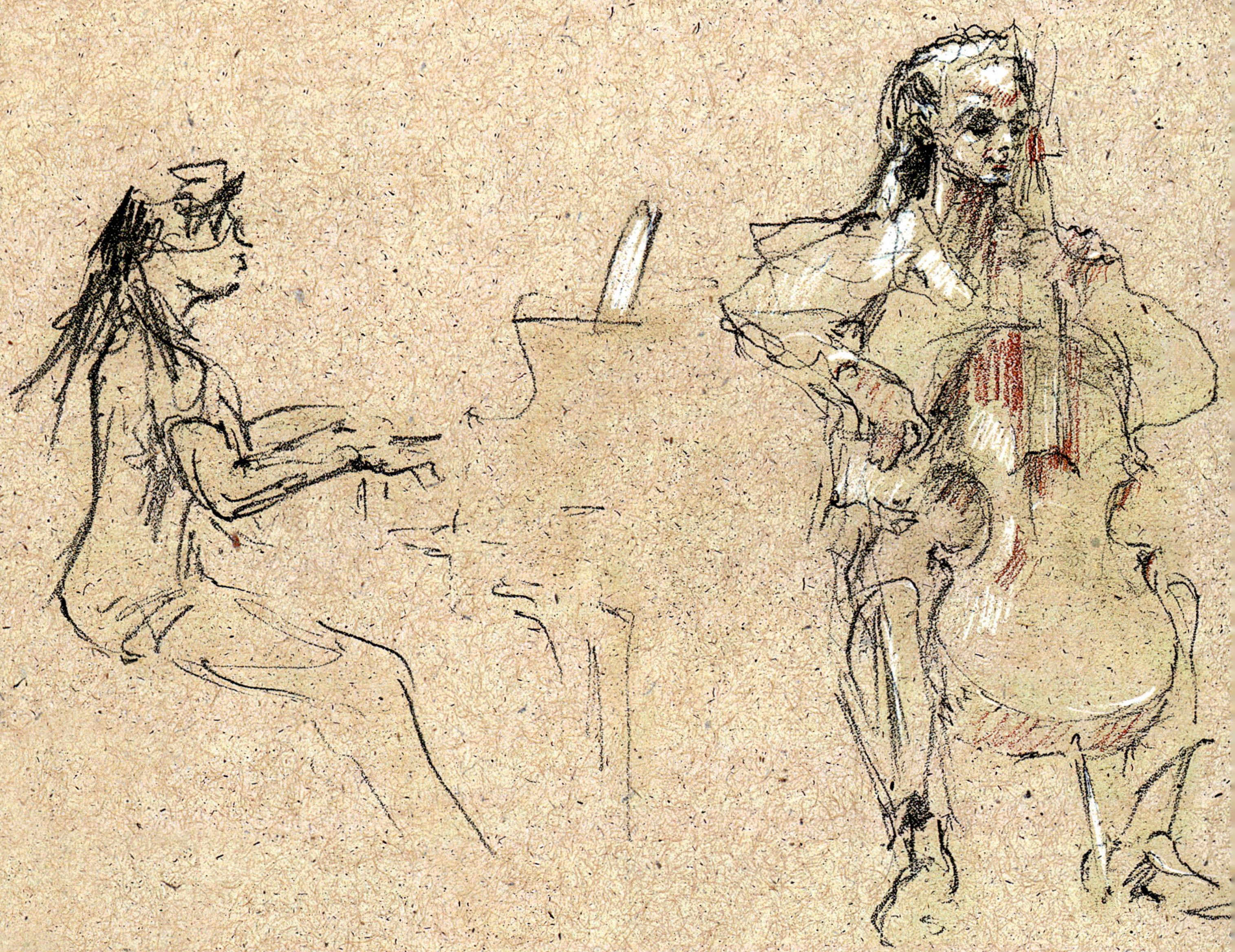

Rostropovich is at a grand piano off stage, while Akiko Hosaki, at a piano on stage, joins Gregory Beaver on the cello in the Prokofiev Symfonia Concertante. Prokofiev had written this piece of music for Rostropovich. (Rostropovich lived with Prokofiev for five years.)

During the lesson Rostropovich played the piano and the cello and regaled the students with the most fascinating stories about his life and his intimate contact with many of the composers that the students were playing, notably Prokofiev and Shostakovich.

Rostropovich played without any music at all. He can play any passage on either instrument. He has it all in his head.

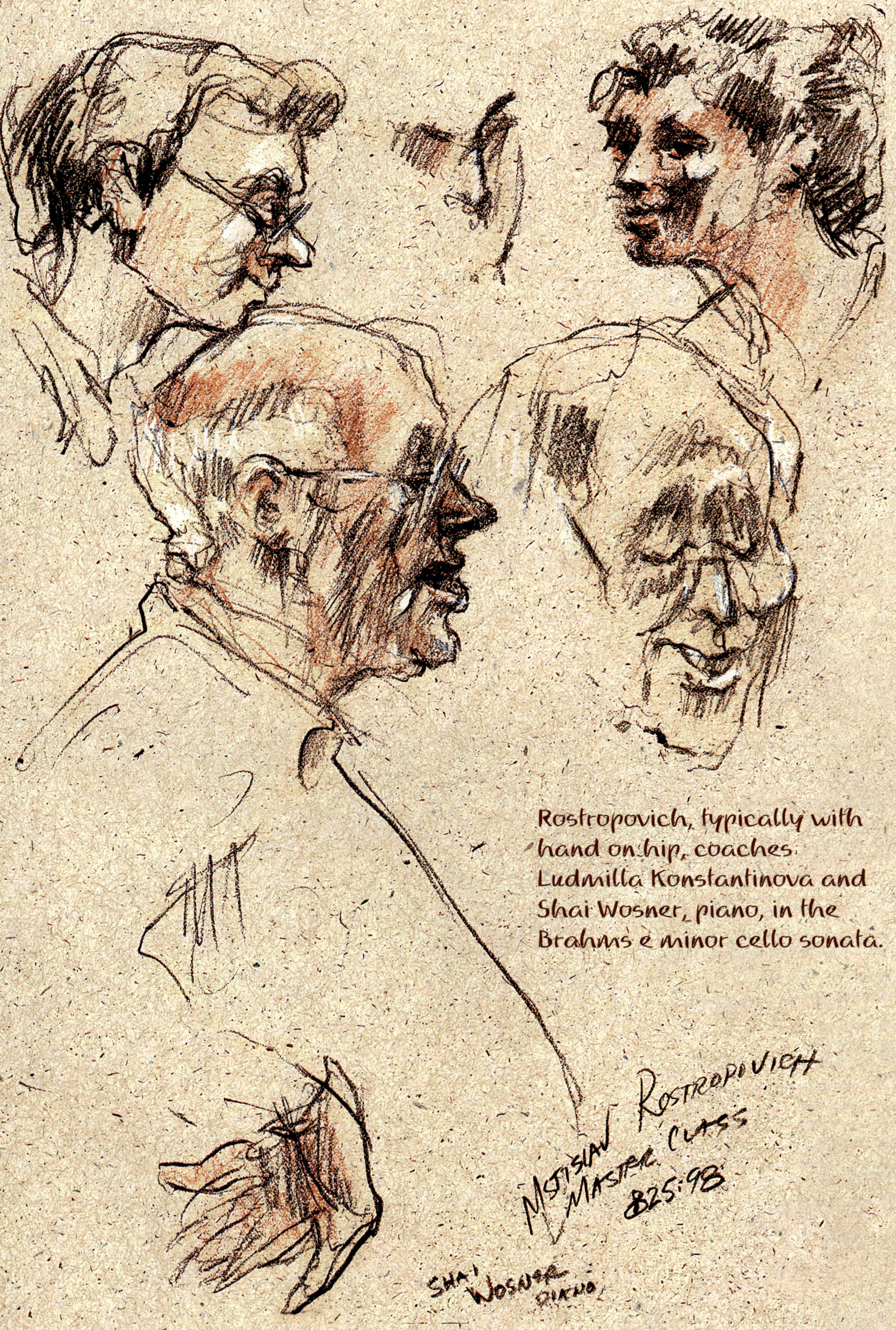

Rostropovich, typically with hand on hip, coaches Ludmilla Konstantinova and Shai Wosner, piano, in the Brahms e minor cello sonata.

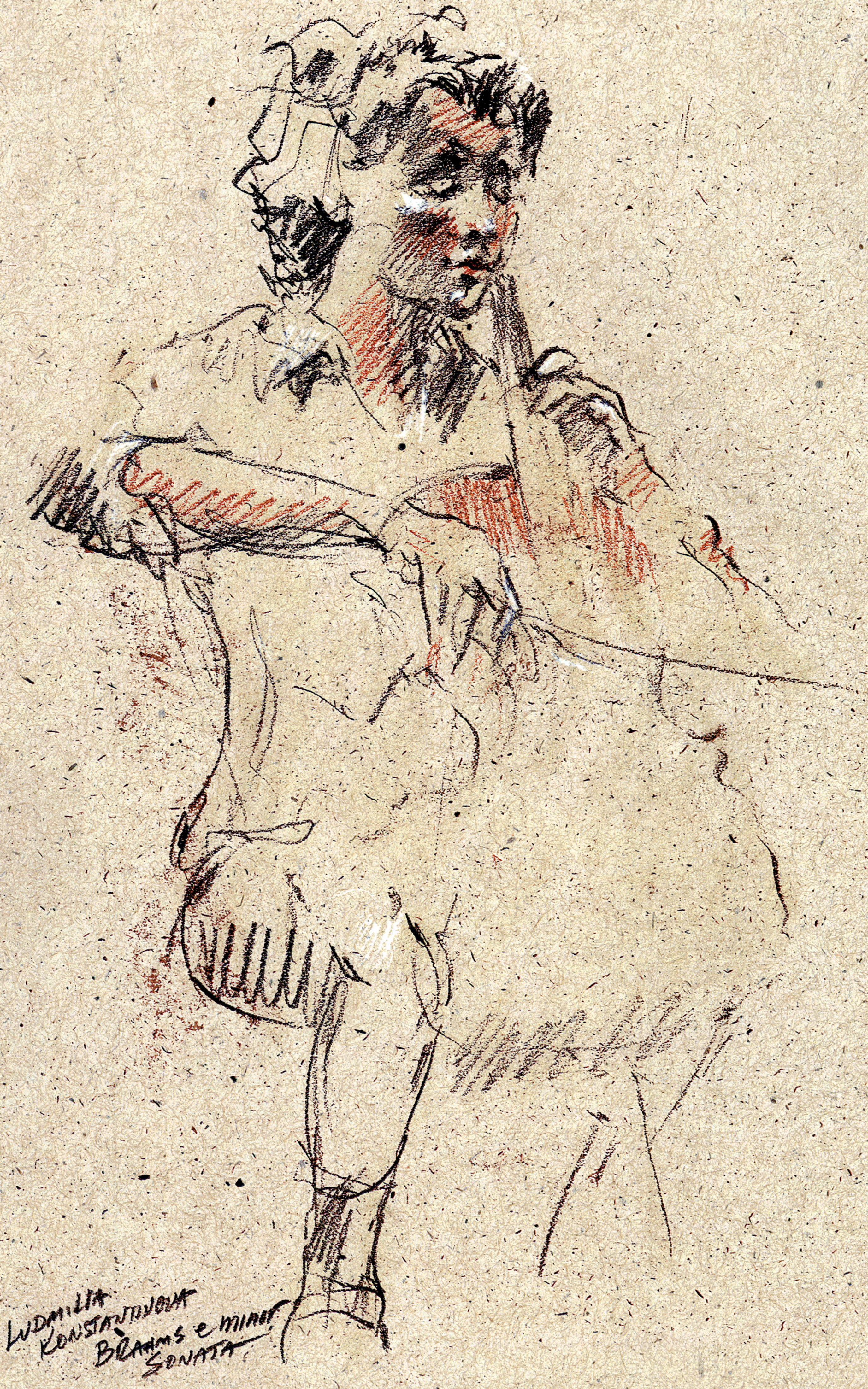
LUDMILLA
KONSTANTINOVA
BRAHMS e minor
SONATA

Master Class on a formidable cello concerto, Bloch's, "Shelomo". Rostropovich gently leads Rapheal Popper-Keiser through some of the more difficult passages.

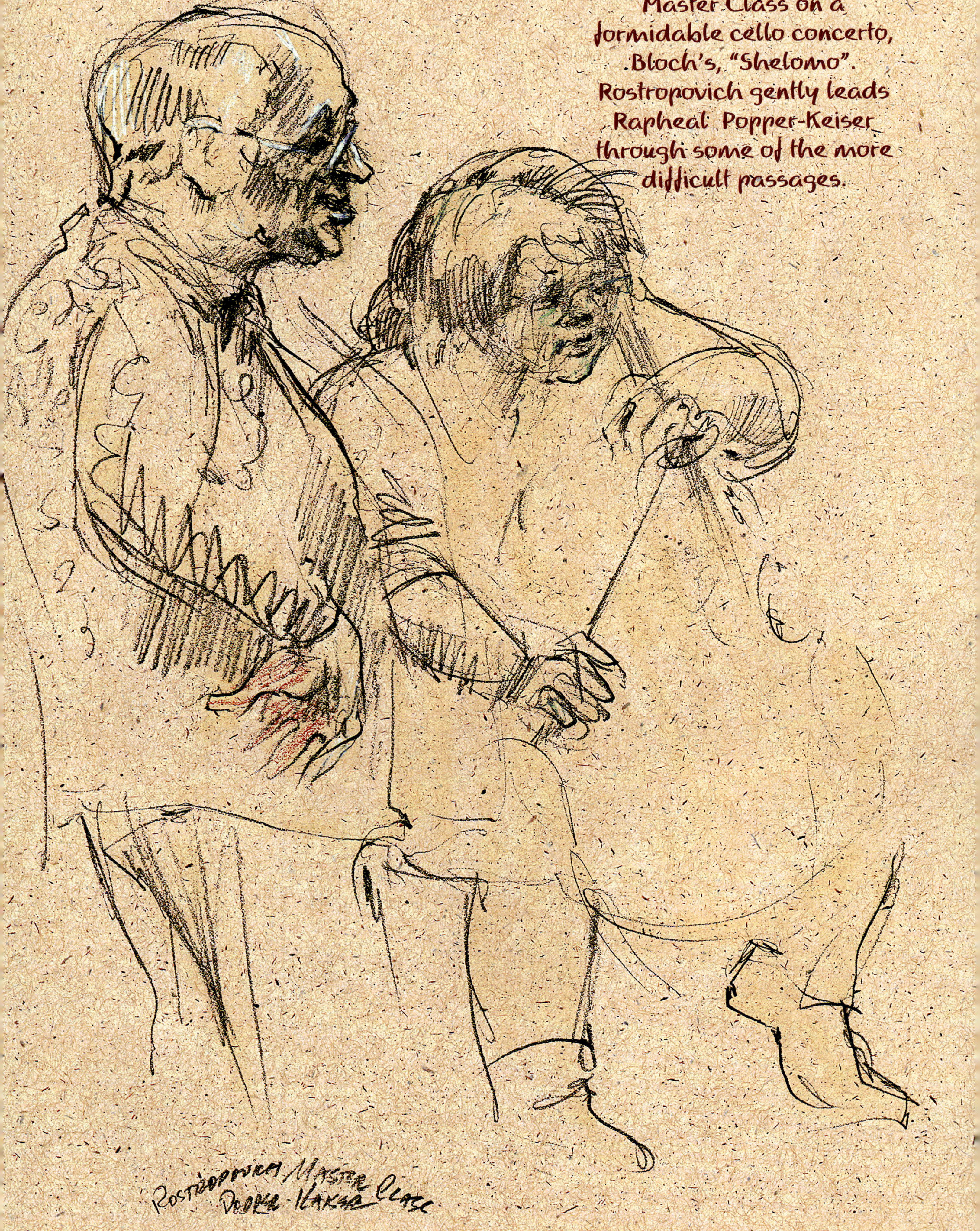

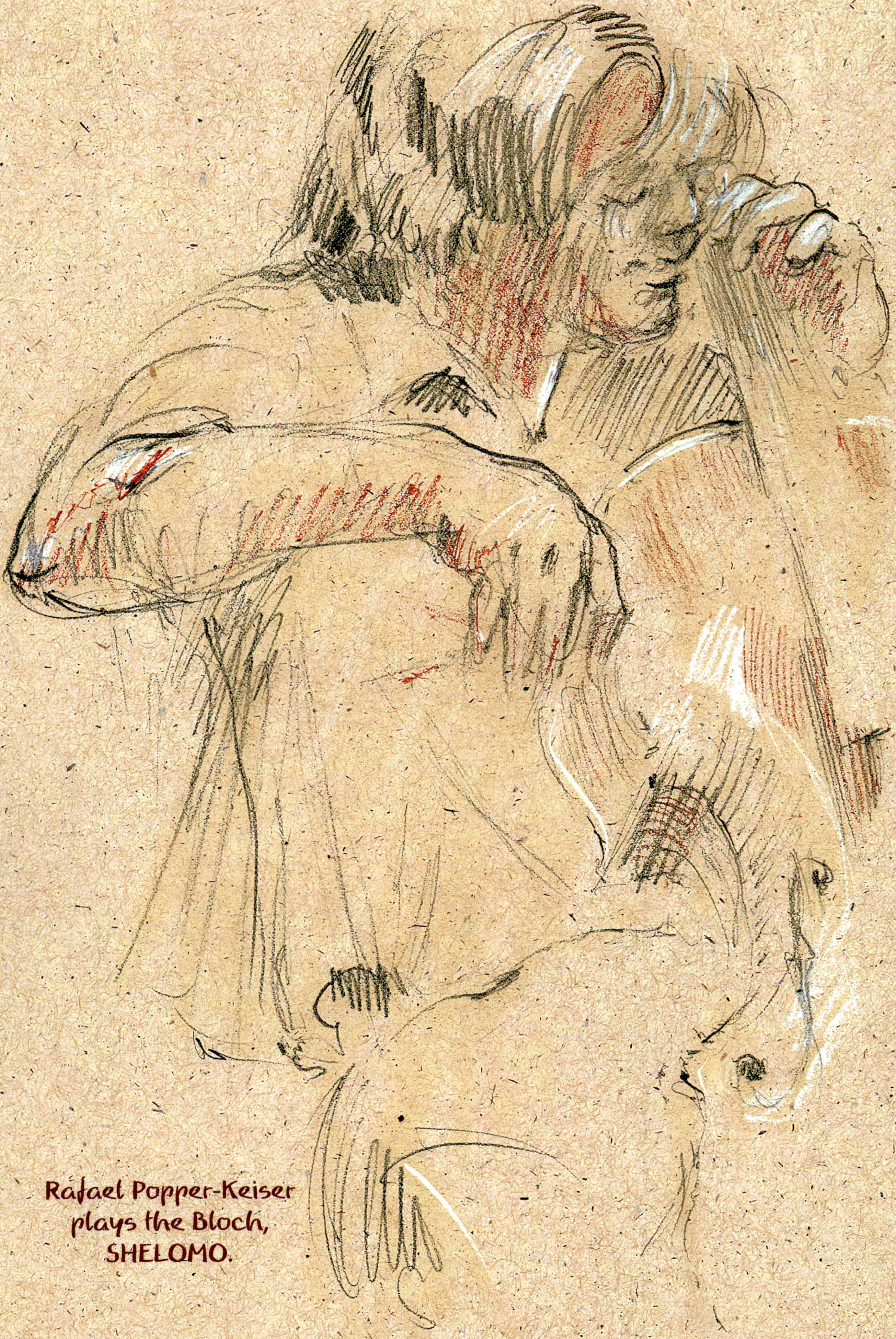

Rafael Popper-Keiser
plays the Bloch,
SHELOMO.

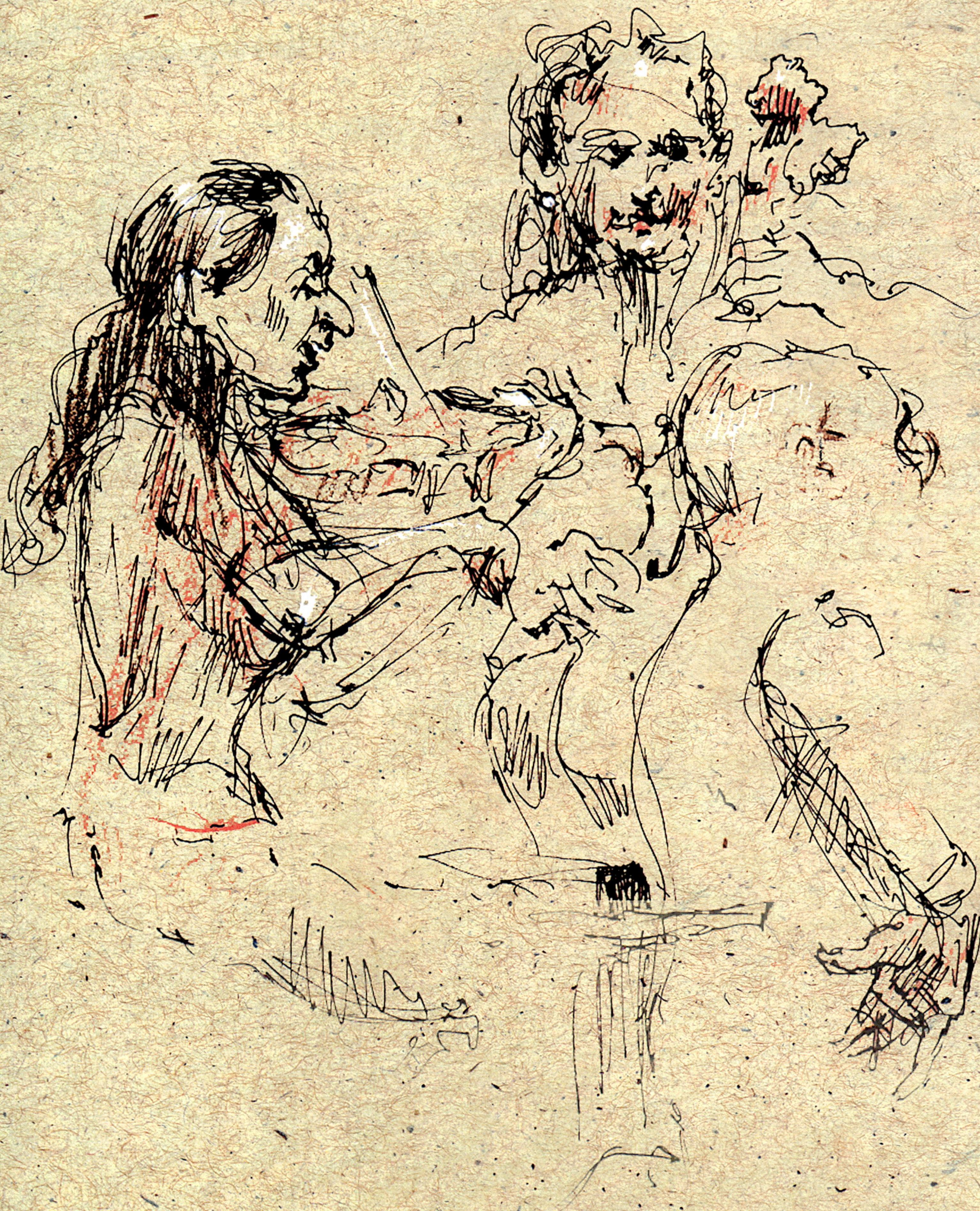

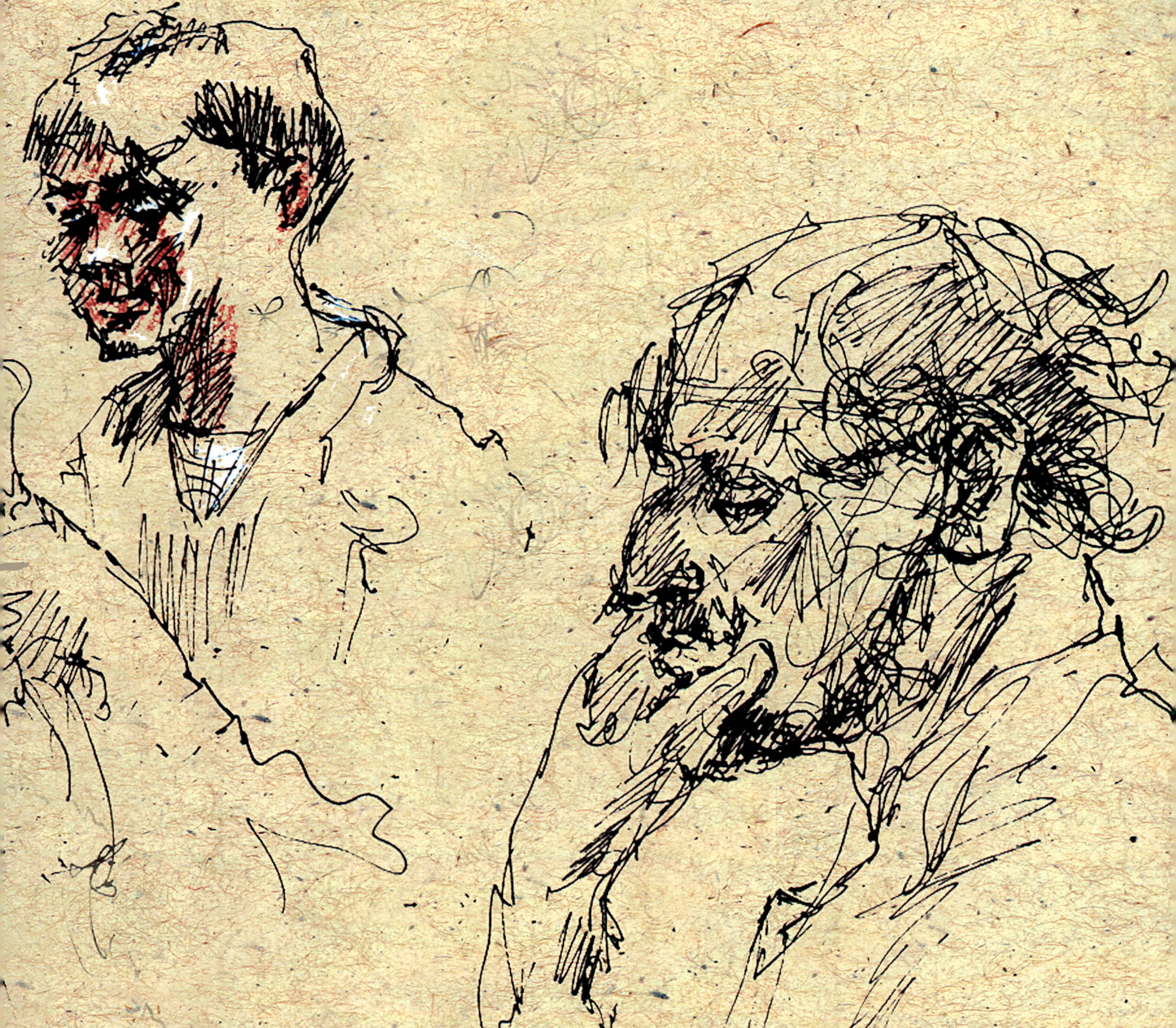

Rostropovich hand on hip gets into the middle of the quartet with Anna Elashvili, violin, Carina Reeves, cello, and Andrew Duckles, viola to discuss their playing of the Shostakovich Quartet No. 3.

He related his experiences with Shostakovich when this Quartet was written that illuminated this hour for both the students and the fortunate listeners.

Michael Zaretsky,a friend and BSO violist stands by to help with any needed translations. Rostropovich didn't need much assistance he is very articulate.

His mental and physical agility are extraordinary. As he told his pertinent stories he would easily leap up on the stage to play a cello passage while standing and then gracefully leap down to play a phrase on the piano.

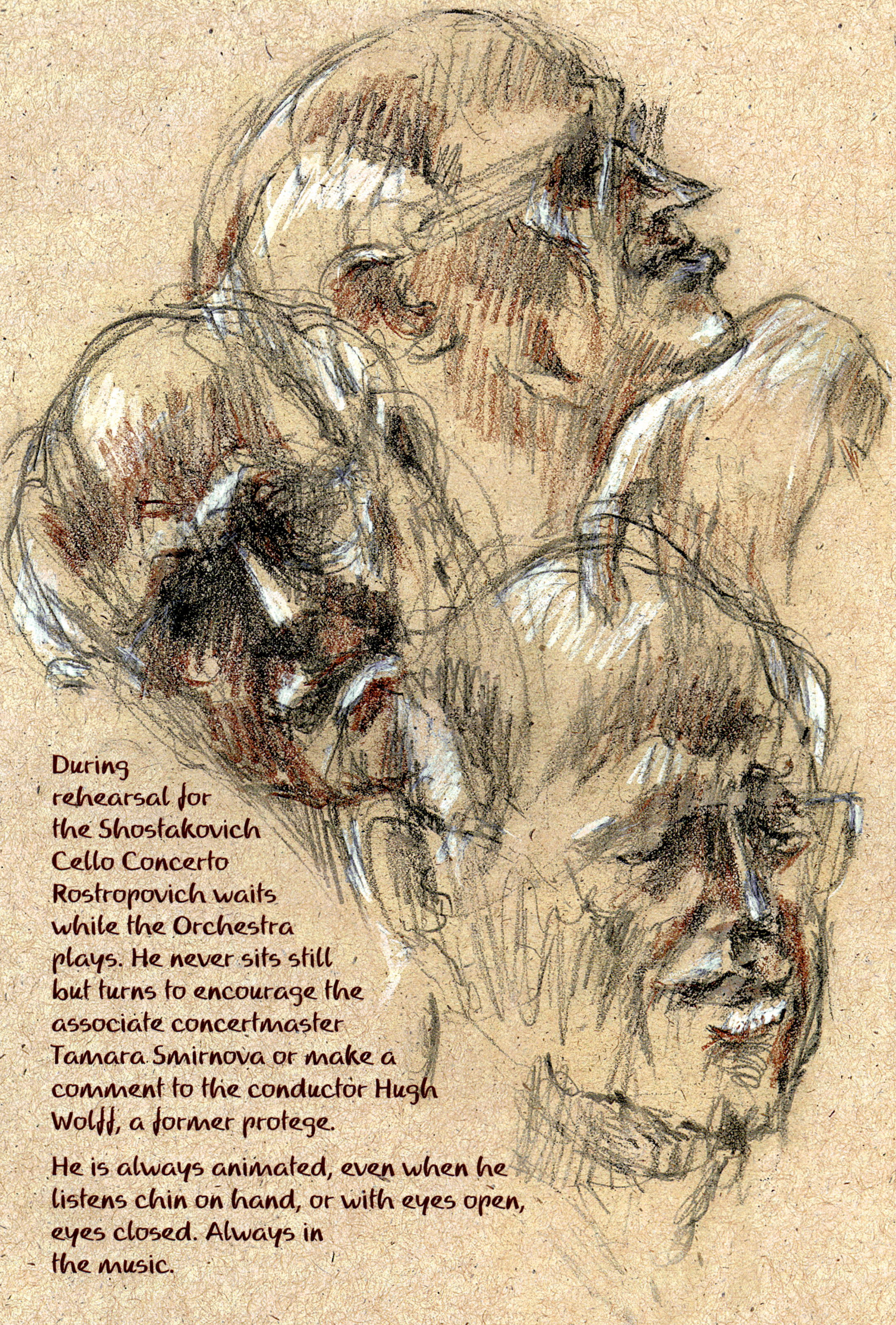

During rehearsal for the Shostakovich Cello Concerto Rostropovich waits while the Orchestra plays. He never sits still but turns to encourage the associate concertmaster Tamara Smirnova or make a comment to the conductor Hugh Wolff, a former protege.

He is always animated, even when he listens chin on hand, or with eyes open, eyes closed. Always in the music.

HUGH WOLFF conducts Rostropovich during a rehearsal for the Shostakovich cello concerto.

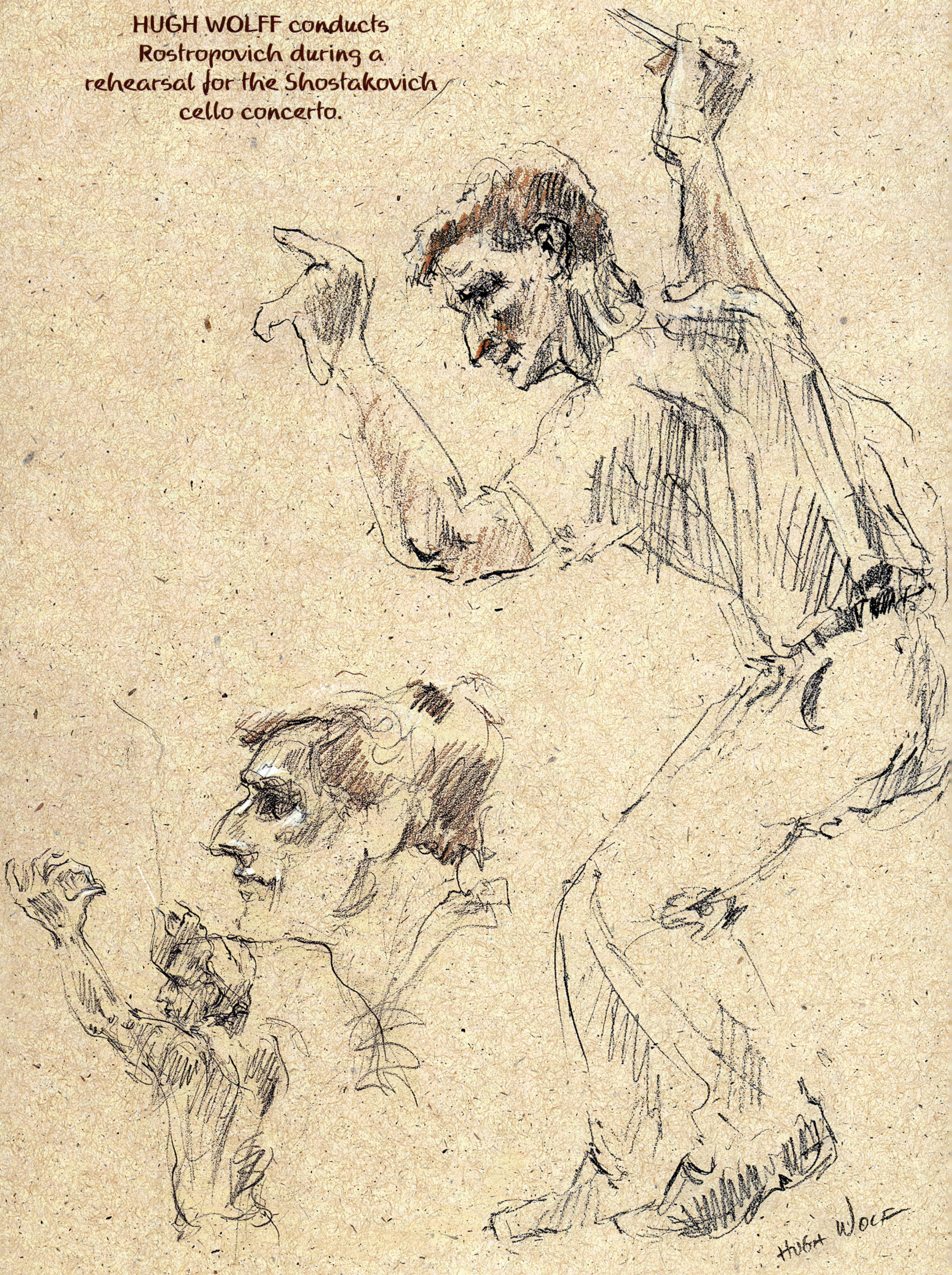

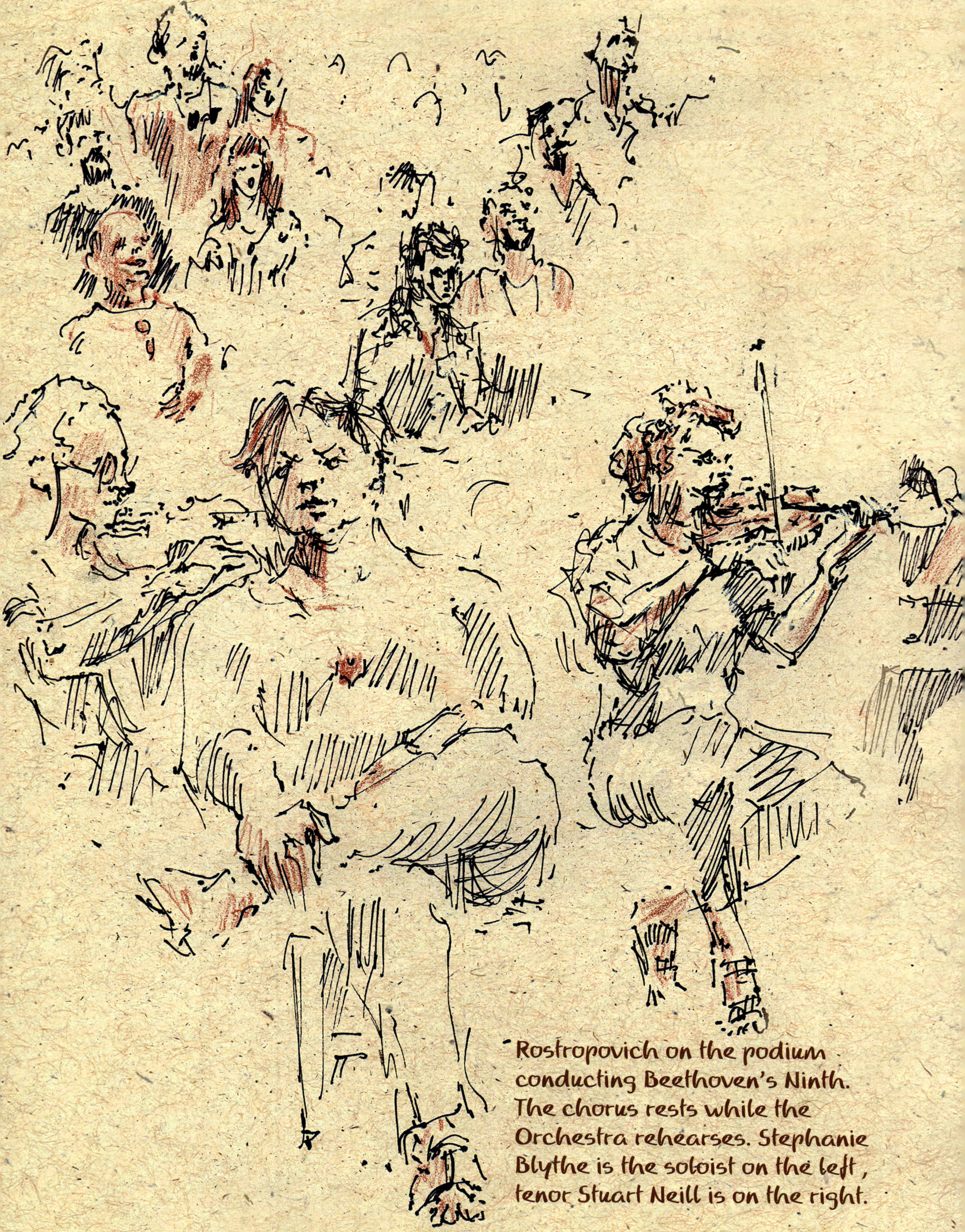

Rostropovich on the podium
conducting Beethoven's Ninth.
The chorus rests while the
Orchestra rehearses. Stephanie
Blythe is the soloist on the left,
tenor Stuart Neill is on the right.

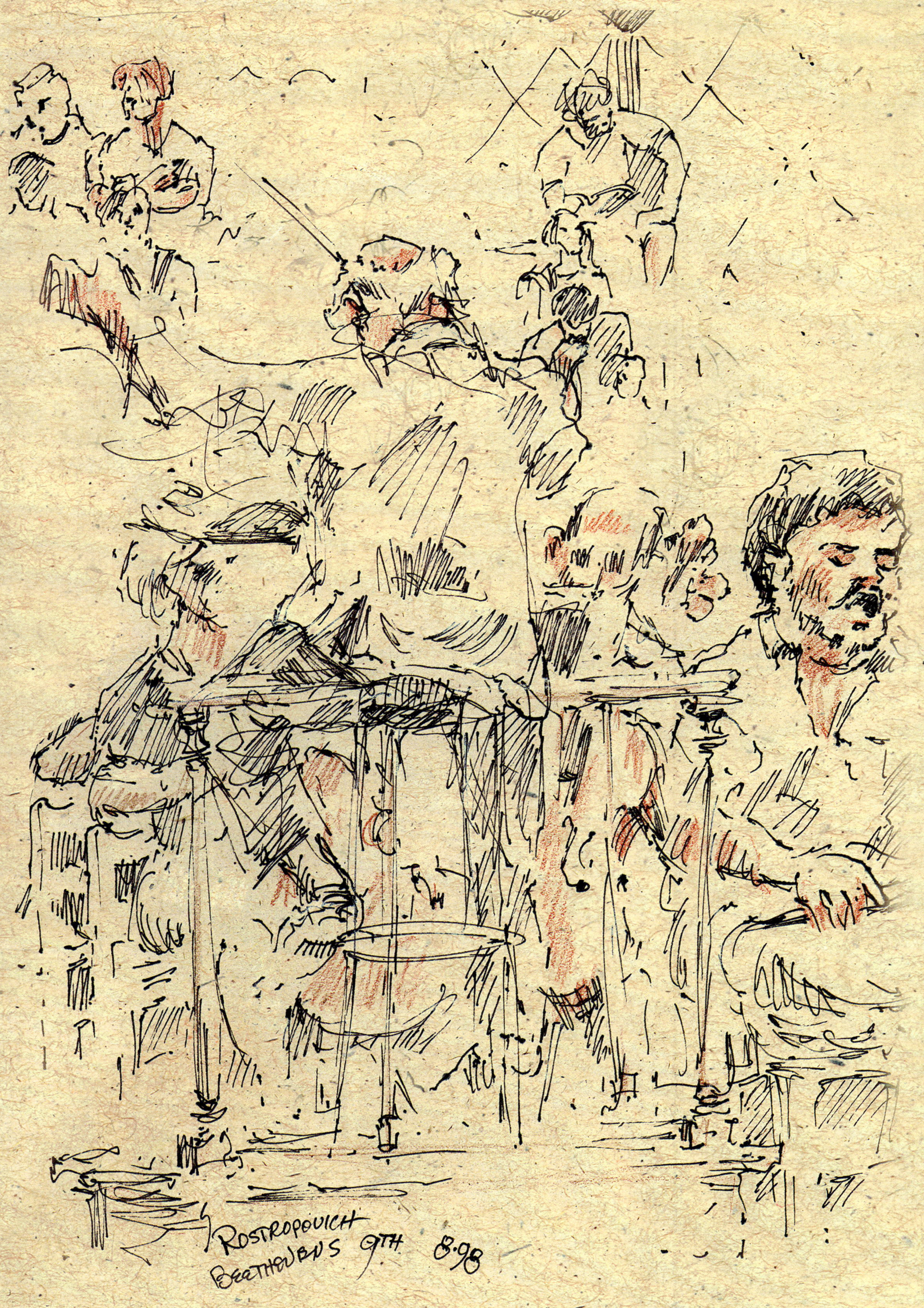
ROSTROPOVICH
BEETHOVENS 9TH 8-98

The Tanglewood Music Center Fellows

The Tanglewood Music Center (TMC) is the international magnet for the world's greatest young talent. Here is a sample of my drawings and watercolors of these gifted young artists.

I plan to issue a separate volume devoted to the myriad sessions of TMC Sunday morning chamber music, evening orchestral performances, rehearsals and master classes that occur throughout each incredible summer.

Each TMC fellow has a story to tell.

Jeff Tomlinson

A Peruvian infant, probably of Inca heritage, is adopted by an American family. He is blind. Jeff Tomlinson, small, dark shining hair and beatific smile is a musical prodigy. He can listen to a piece of music, whether it is a Brahms trio or a Beethoven sonata, and he can play it! Truly an overwhelming "sight to see." He is at ease and performs with great sensitivity.

Here he is playing a piano sonata.

On the following pages he is at the piano in a full dress tuxedo, a bit large, doing the Kreutzer sonata with Biliana Voutchkova, a handsome and gifted Bulgarian violinist. It was a privilege to witness this miracle, and there were few dry eyes in the audience when it ended.

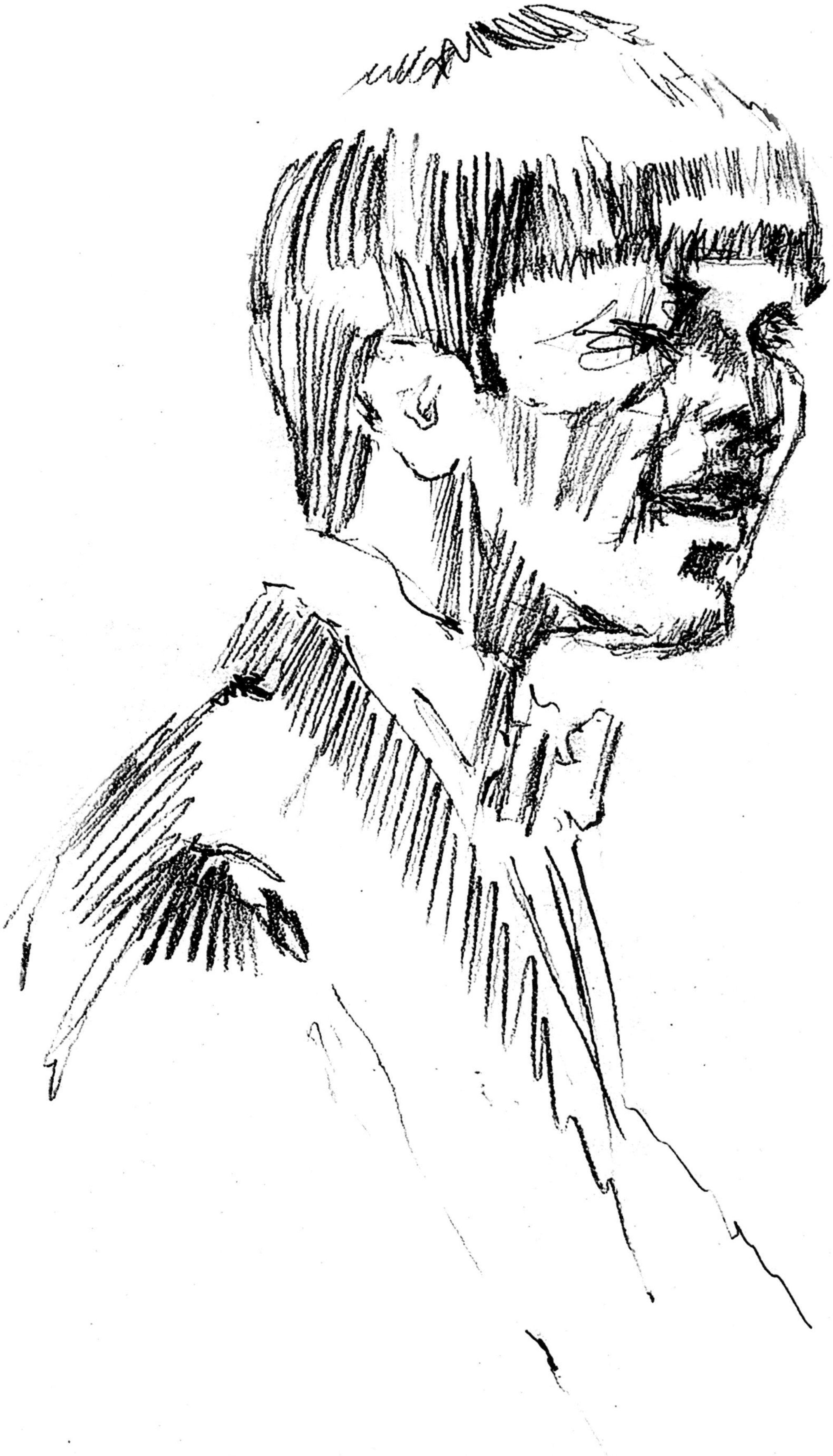

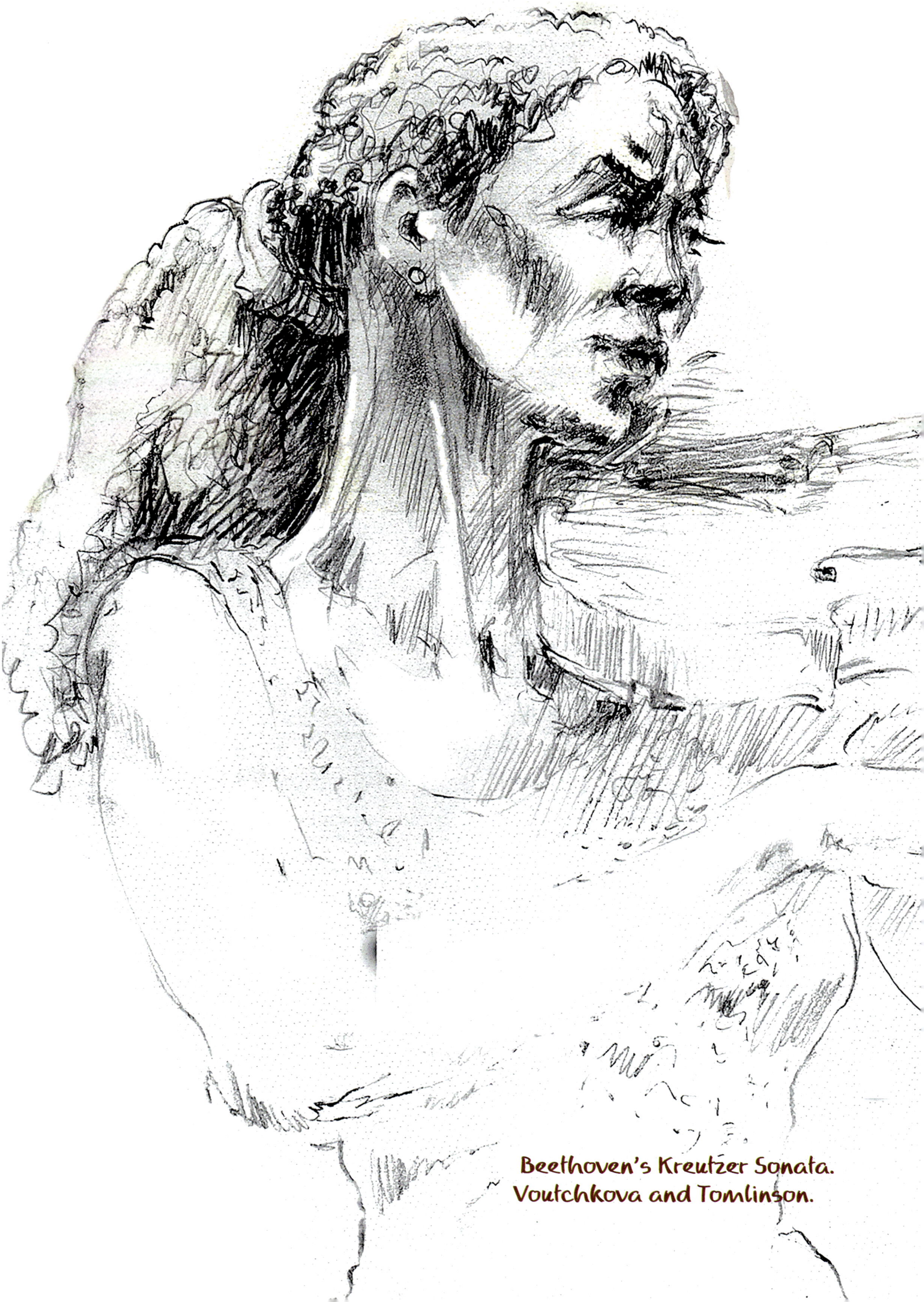

Beethoven's Kreutzer Sonata.
Voutchkova and Tomlinson.

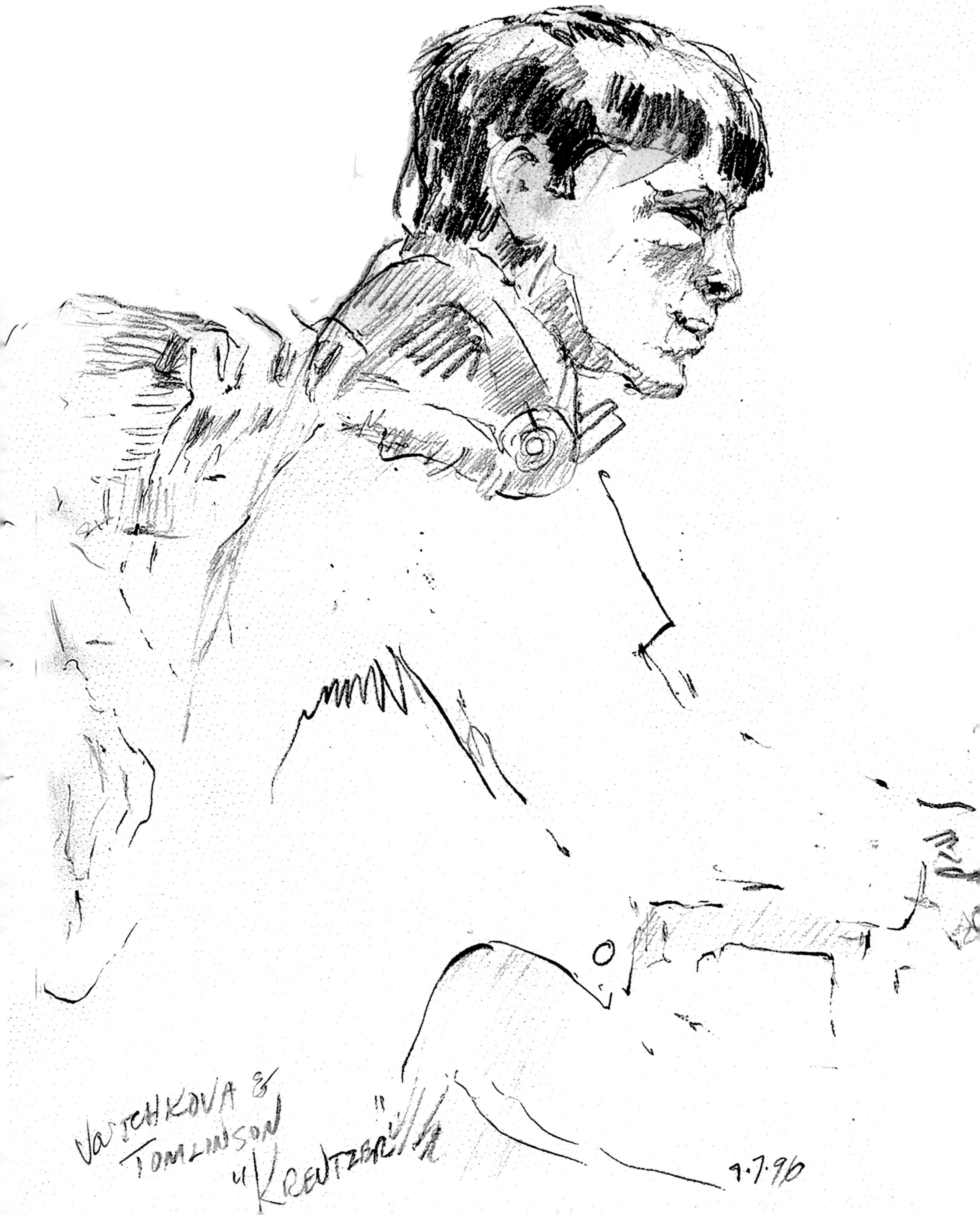
VAJTCHKOVA &
TOMLINSON
v KREUTZER
9.7.96

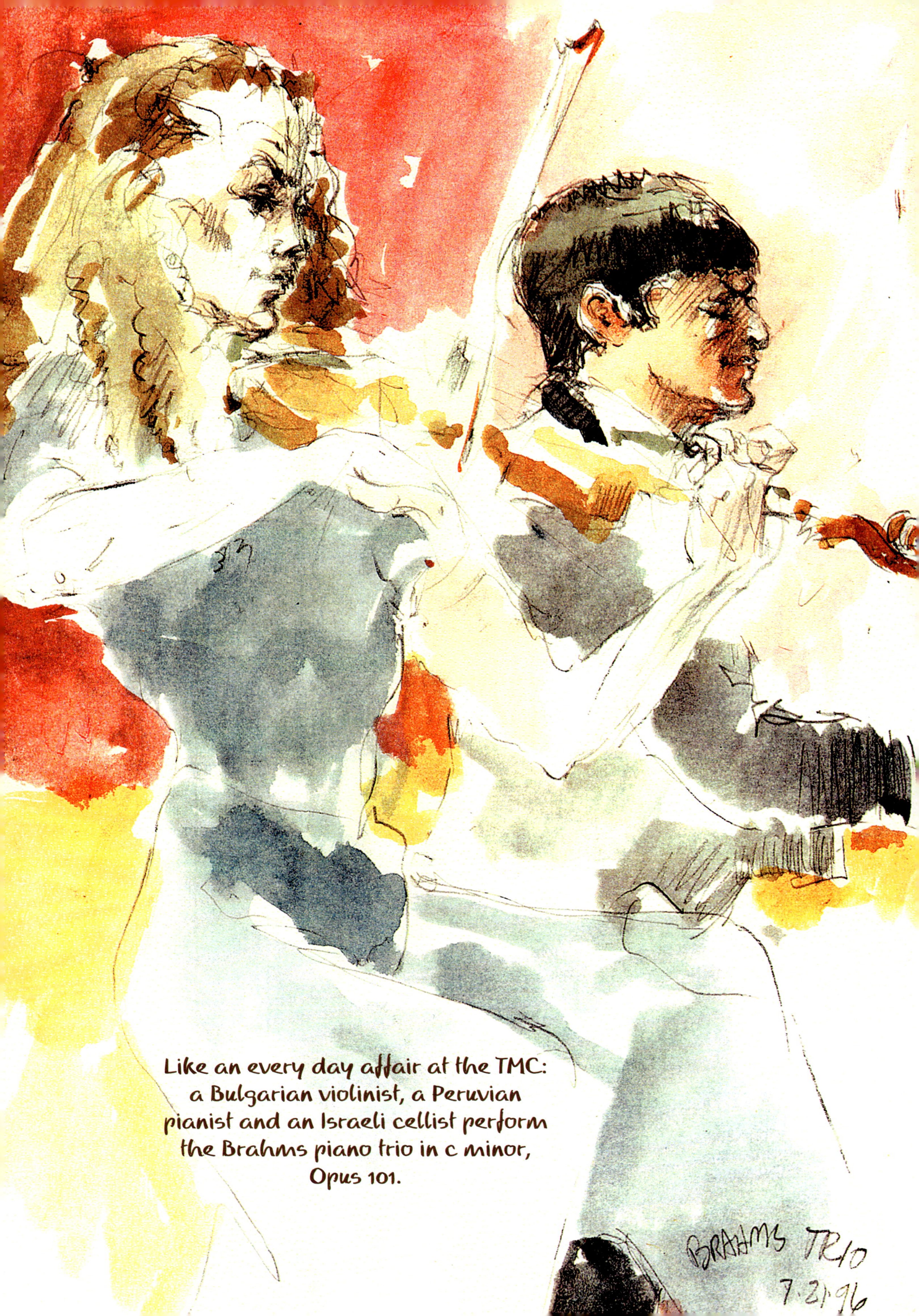

Like an every day affair at the TMC:
a Bulgarian violinist, a Peruvian
pianist and an Israeli cellist perform
the Brahms piano trio in c minor,
Opus 101.

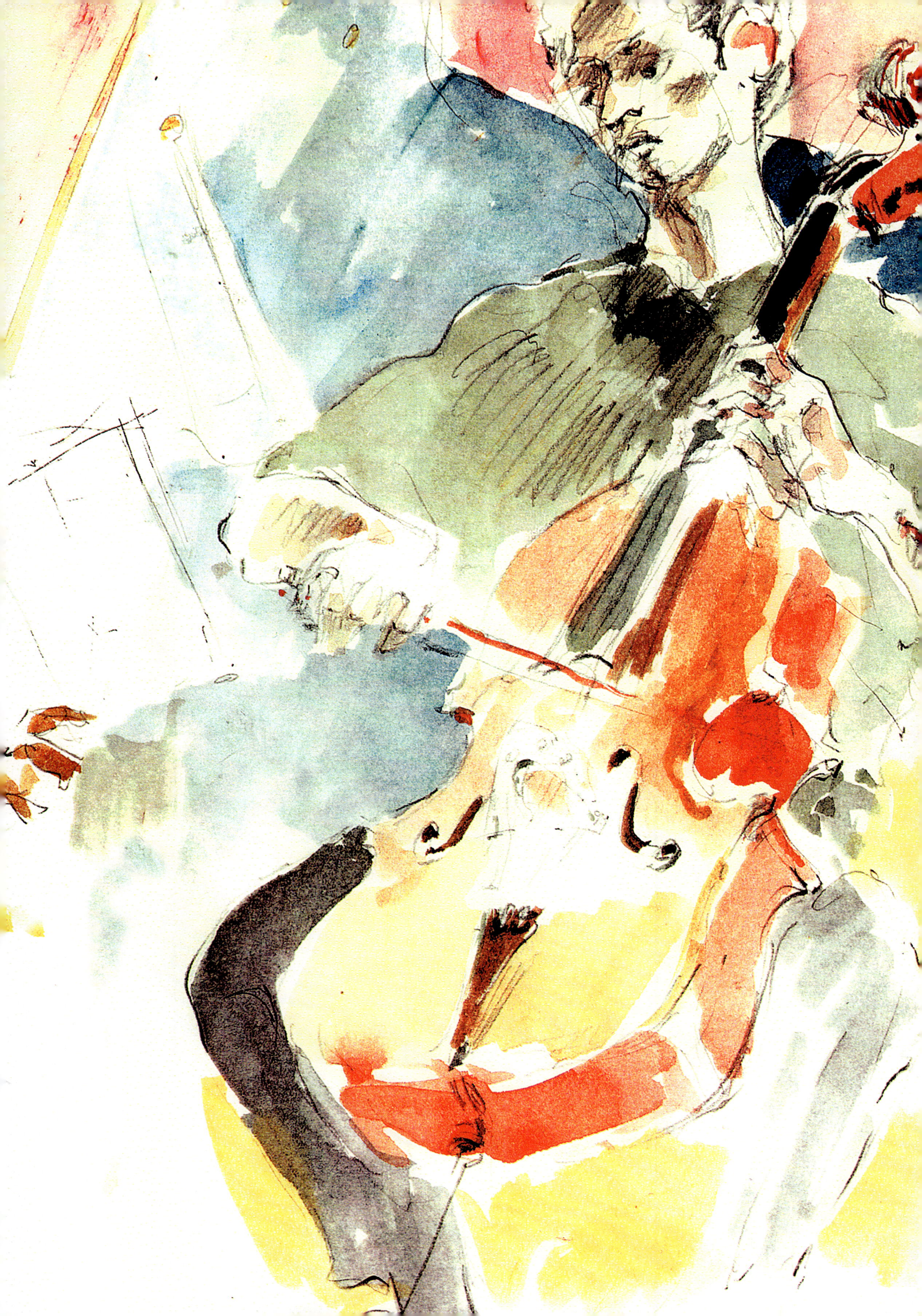

TMC Fellow Rafael Popper-Keizer

There are always a few of the TMC fellows that seem to creep into more of my drawings. Partly because of their great talent, partly because of the way they behave on stage, their persona, and the way they look. Whatever it is, Rafael Popper-Keizer, a brilliant and gifted young cellist from the Berkeley area in California, has been invited to Tanglewood a number of times.

His dress code is very distinctive. He wears a black raincoat, a black turtleneck, black pants, heavy black shoes, and a black vest. And he wears them all the time unless he has to dress up in a tuxedo for a performance, or it is very hot.

Here he is playing with the Tanglewood Music Center Orchestra as principal cellist. He literally dances as he plays and causes my line to dance along with him.

Rafael was asked to substitute for the soloist, YoYo Ma, during rehearsals for Don Quixote. On the next page he is in a black tee shirt. It was very hot. Opposite is a drawing of him on the podium they set up for the soloist. Seiji Ozawa was conducting and Rafael was a very credible replacement.

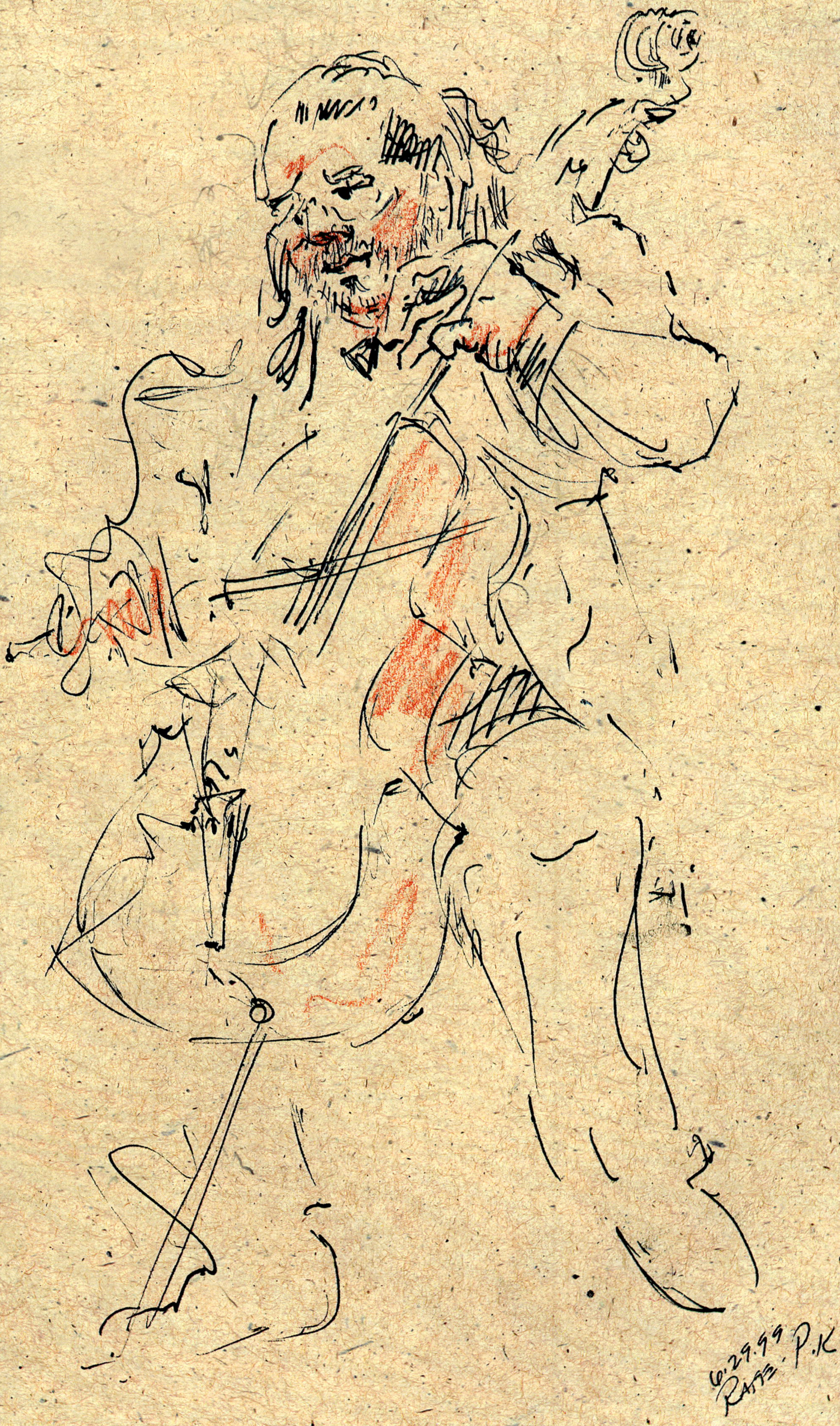
6.29.99
P.K

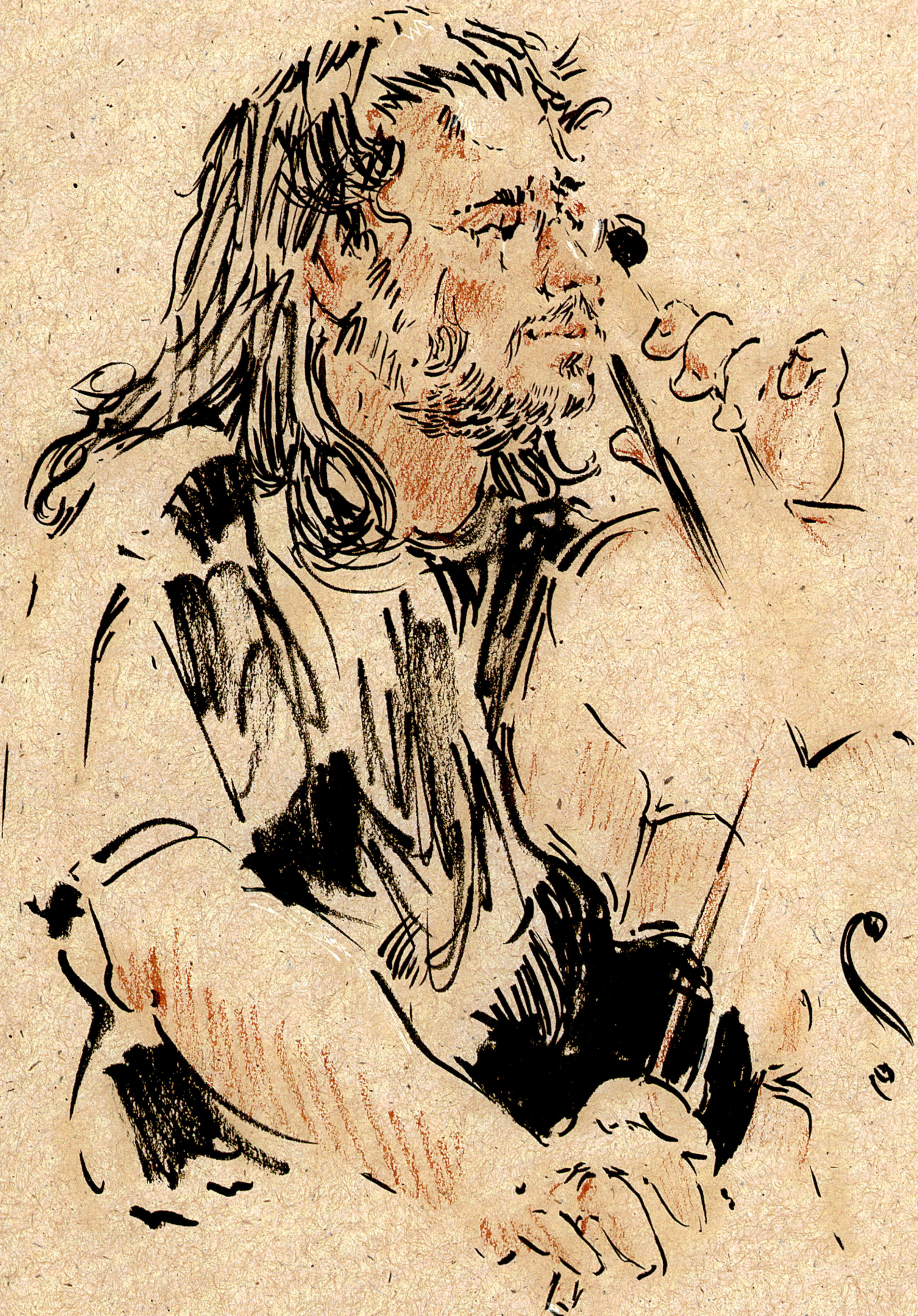

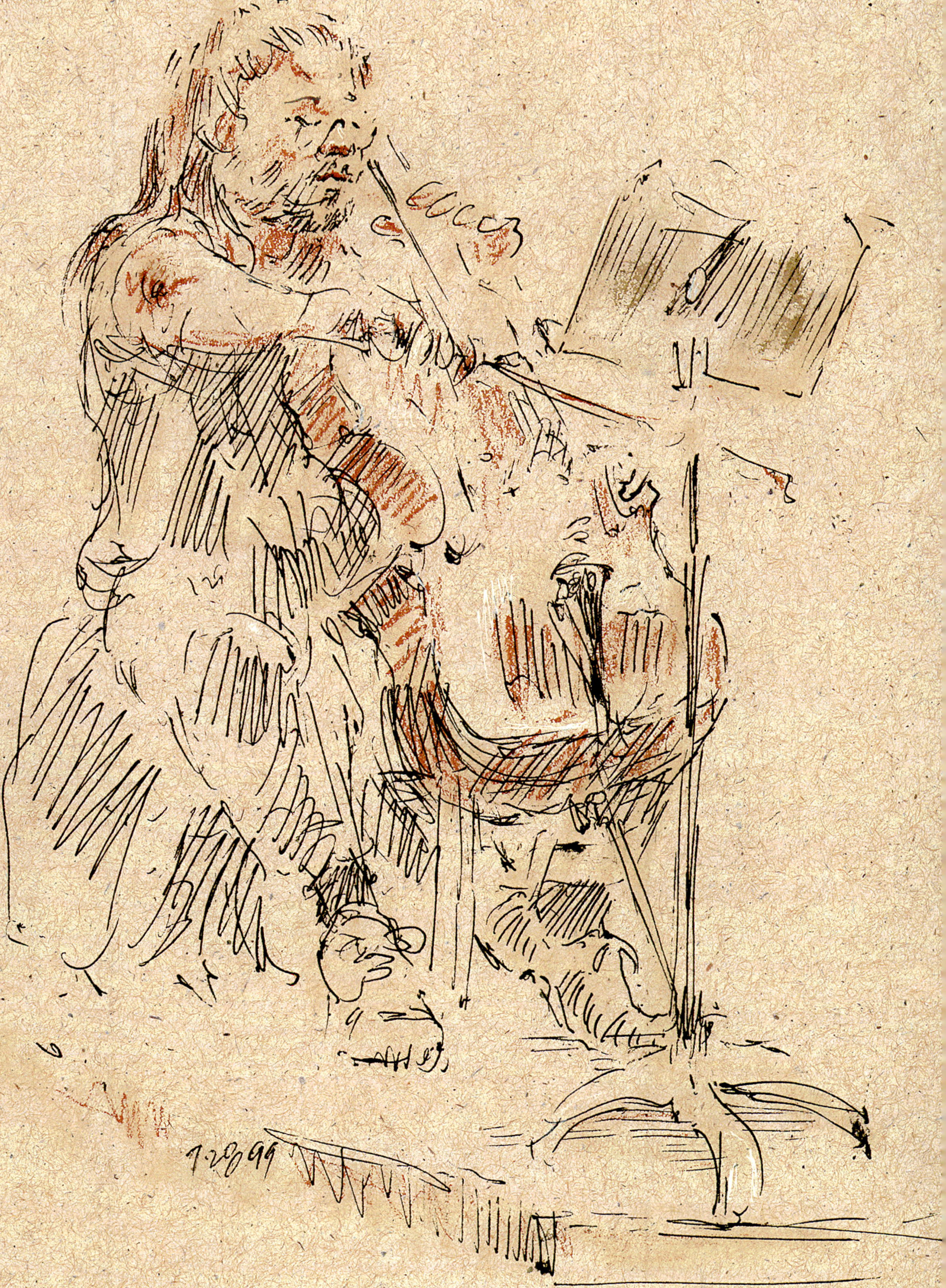
7·28·99

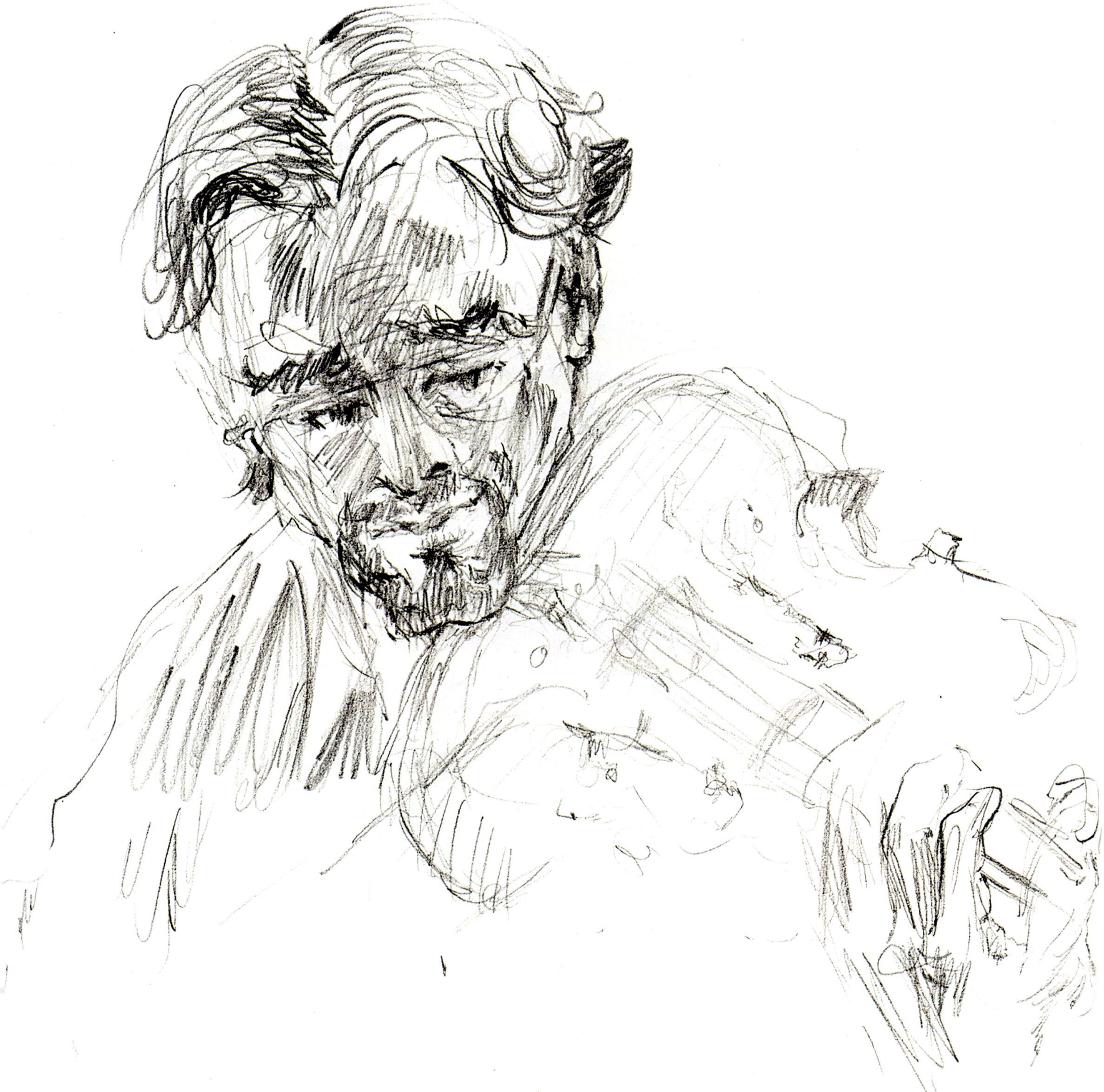

This is part of a set of drawings of a TMC string quartet in rehearsal with Rafael and a fine violist, Dimitri Koustanovich.

Rafael is wearing his raincoat.

What a marvelous opportunity to hear these young artists at the outset of their career.

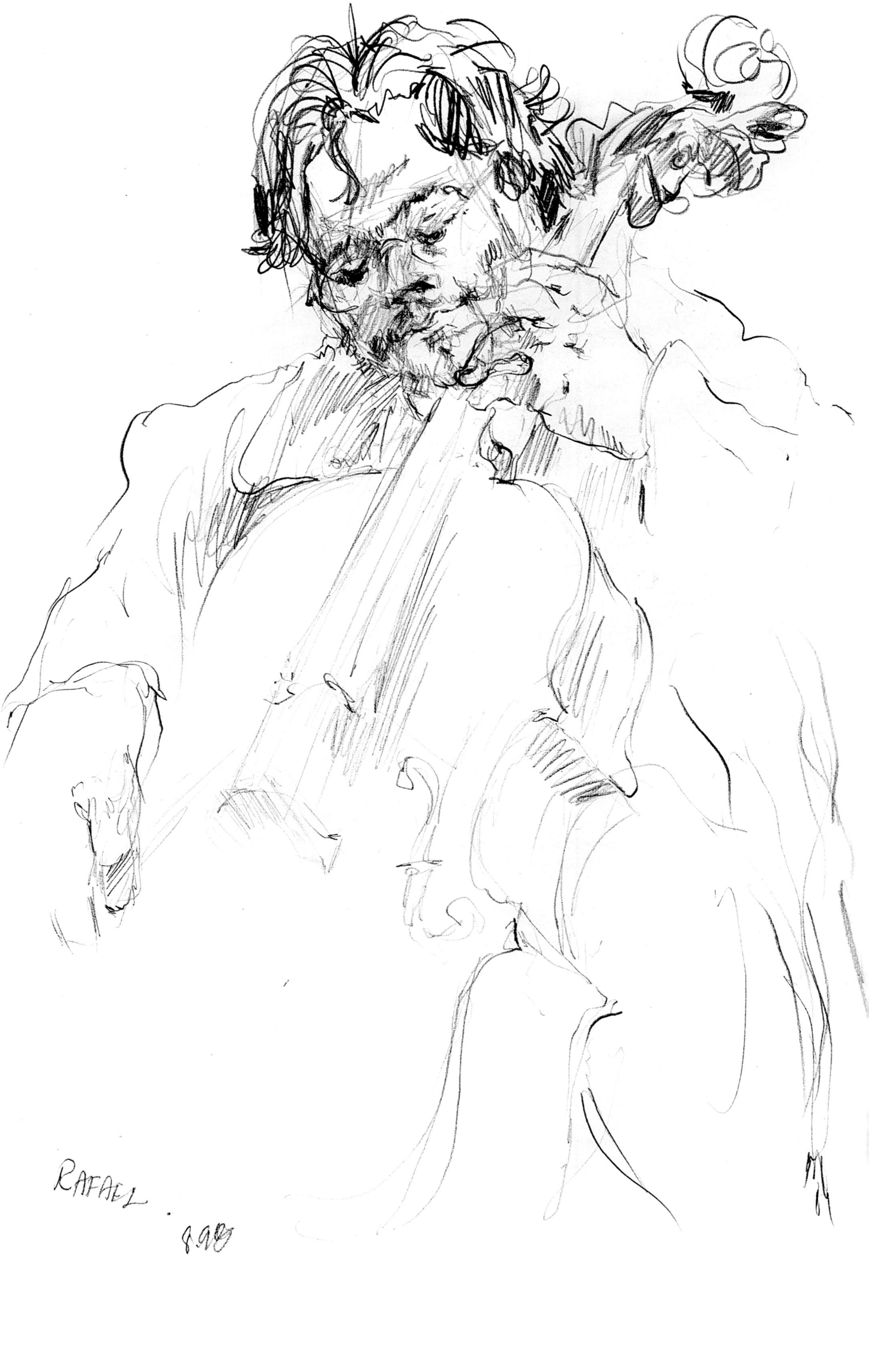
RAFAEL
8.98

TMC Fellow Nick Tzavaras

This was a quick drawing that I really enjoyed. It's of Nick Tzavaras playing the cello part of the Haydn E-flat trio. It was done with a minimum amount of lines. You will have to find the cello. It is growing out of, and is part of his head and body, as it should be. I did it rapidly because the section that they were playing was also quite rapid, which moves my hand along. Nick was playing a very delicate passage on the cello and he wanted the touch and the sound to be very light and sweet.

He's playing fairly high up on the fingerboard as you can see. You'll notice he's holding the bow between the thumb and forefinger. His middle finger is lifted up off the bow. Of course, most people are not going to notice this. Since I play the cello I watch carefully for these little tricks.

In order to release the weight of the hand, one of the things that some cellists do is to lift one or two fingers off the cello bow. That's what Nick is doing at this time so he can sort of fly along. You'll notice his eyes are looking across at the other two musicians because he's in the music, involved in it, and I think what I like about the drawing is its delicacy, its immediacy; and the attempt through line to impart this rapid, light, presto passage in the music.

Nick gained some additional notoriety because of a PBS documentary about his mother, the famous Harlem music teacher. It included Nick and his brother playing trios with his mother. The documentary was followed by the film about her work, The Music Teacher, featuring Meryl Streep.

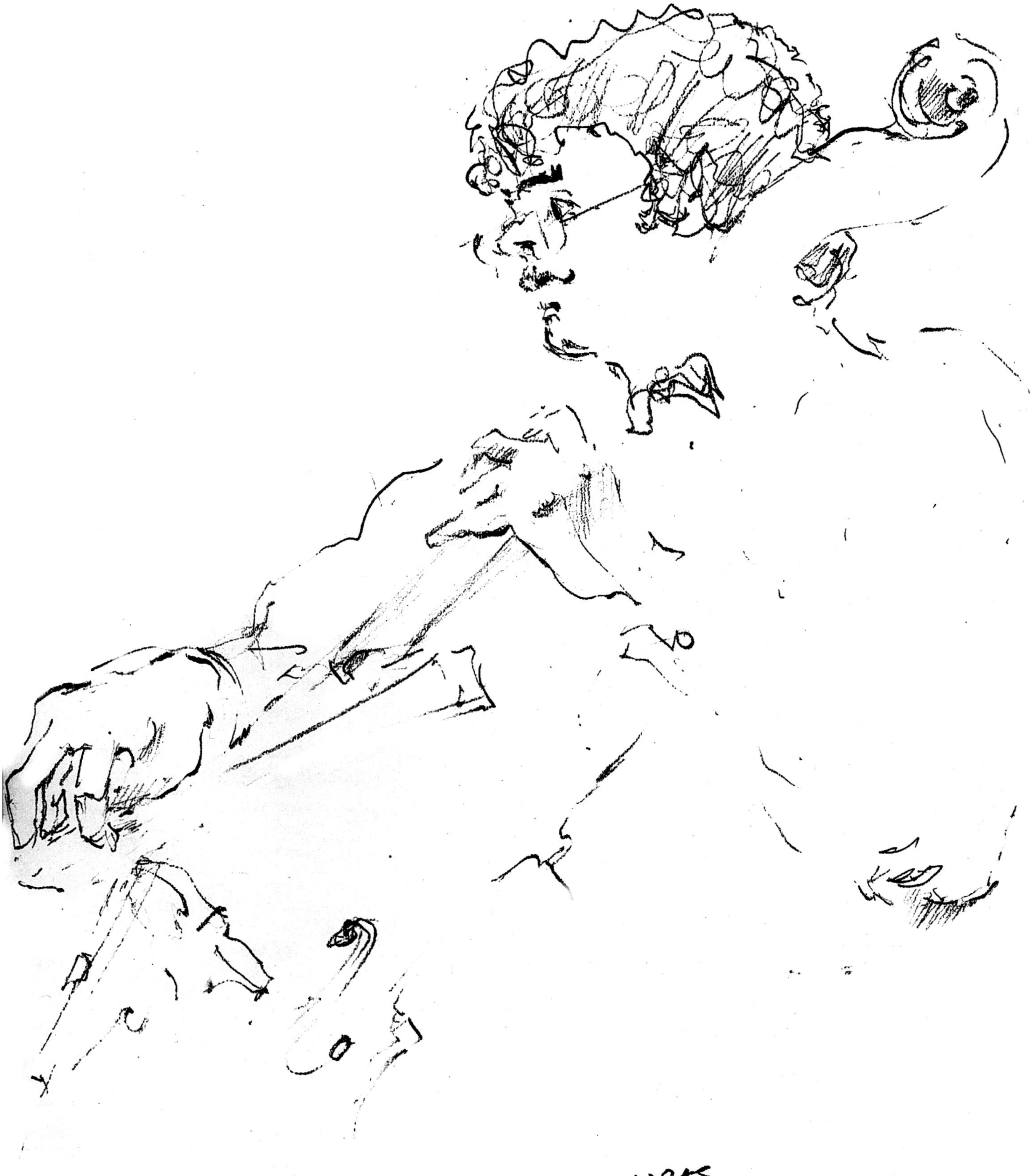

KENYON ab TRIO 11.29 NICK TZAVARAS

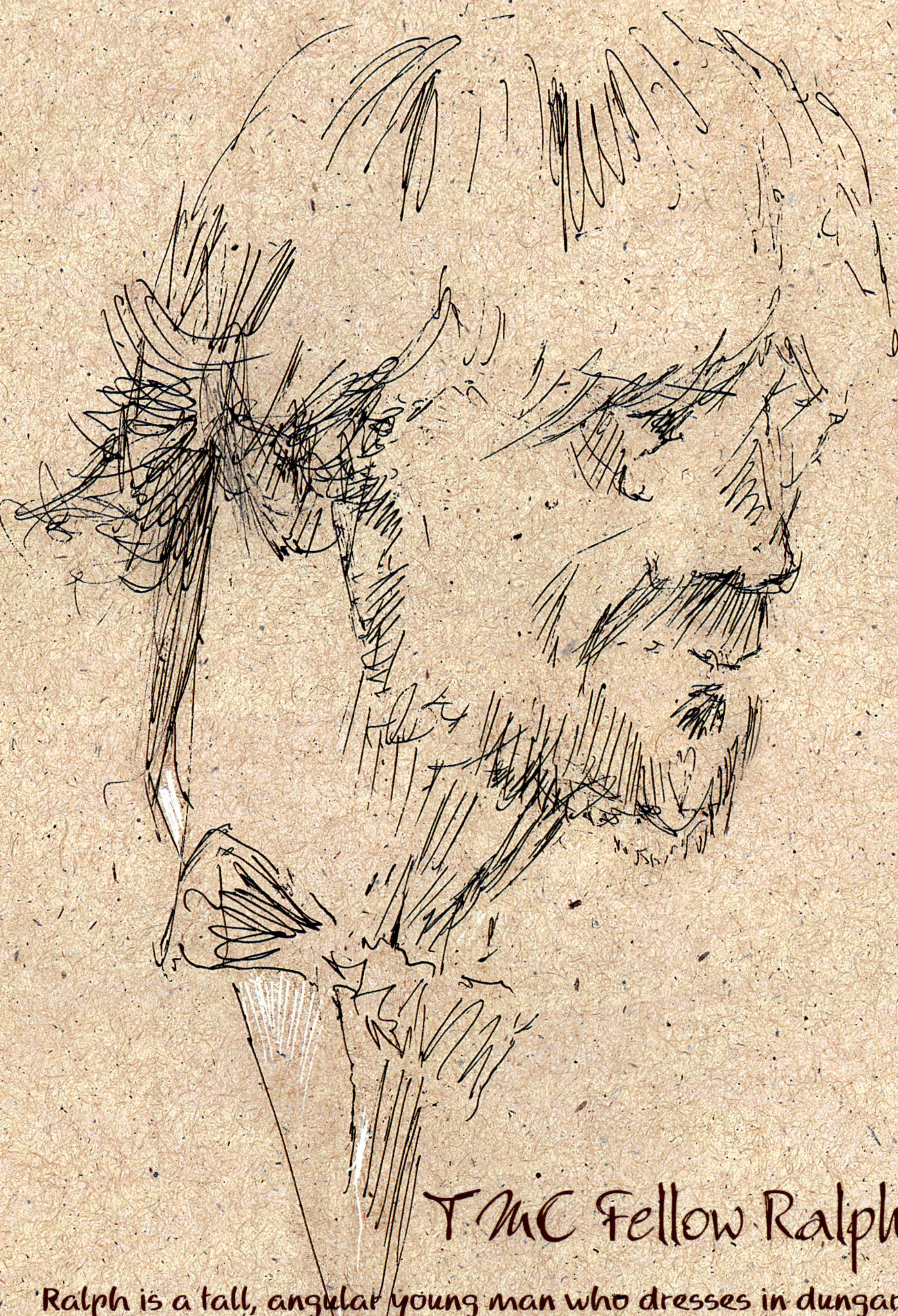

TMC Fellow Ralph Allen

Ralph is a tall, angular young man who dresses in dungarees and a colored vest from Guatemala. On the opposite page he is in a quartet rehearsal. Above, Ralph in a tuxedo playing with the orchestra and on the next page as concertmaster with the Gustave Mahler Youth Orchestra that came to visit and play together with the TMC fellows. Ralph has been at Tanglewood several times and is a gifted violinist with a particularly strong personality.

I have literally hundreds of TMC fellow drawings that will be included in a future volume of Drawing Music, devoted exclusively to them.

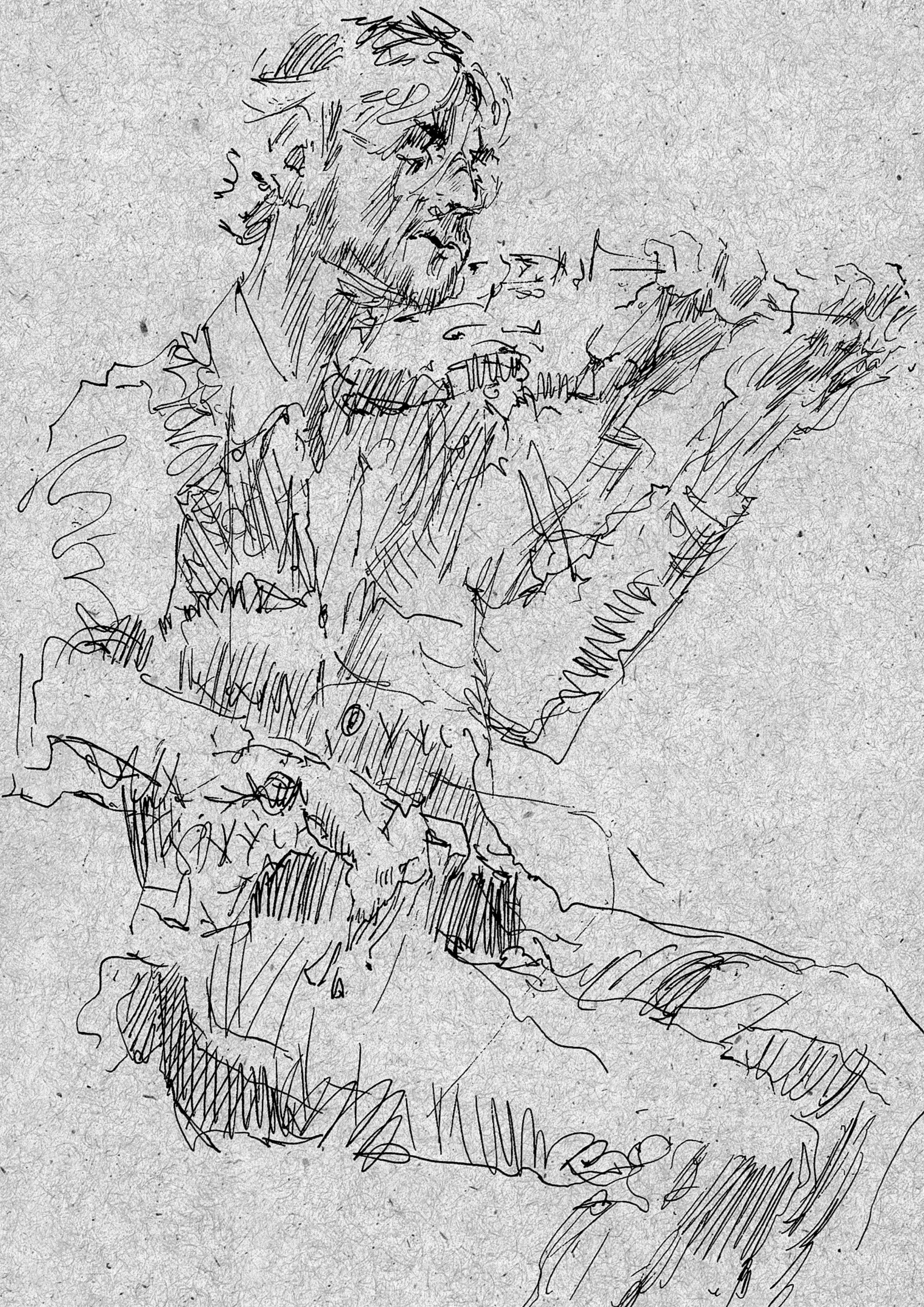

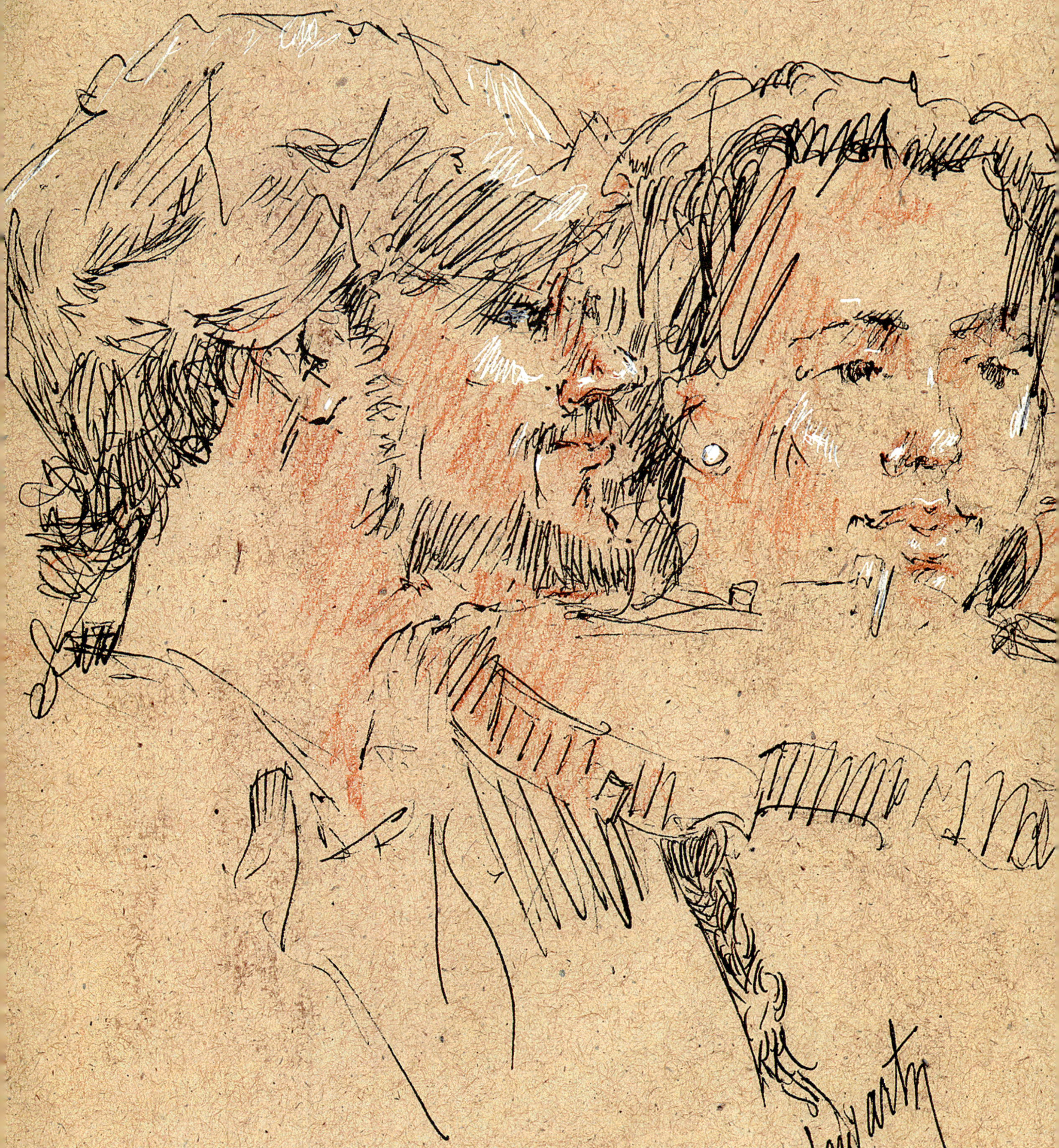

Joel Smirnoff is sitting on the podium below Seiji Ozawa, who is conducting. Joel is passing on little hints and comments from Ozawa and notes he has made to the violinists on how they should be handling some of the passages in the Mahler Symphony.

Schwartz
7-28-99

RALPH ALLEN

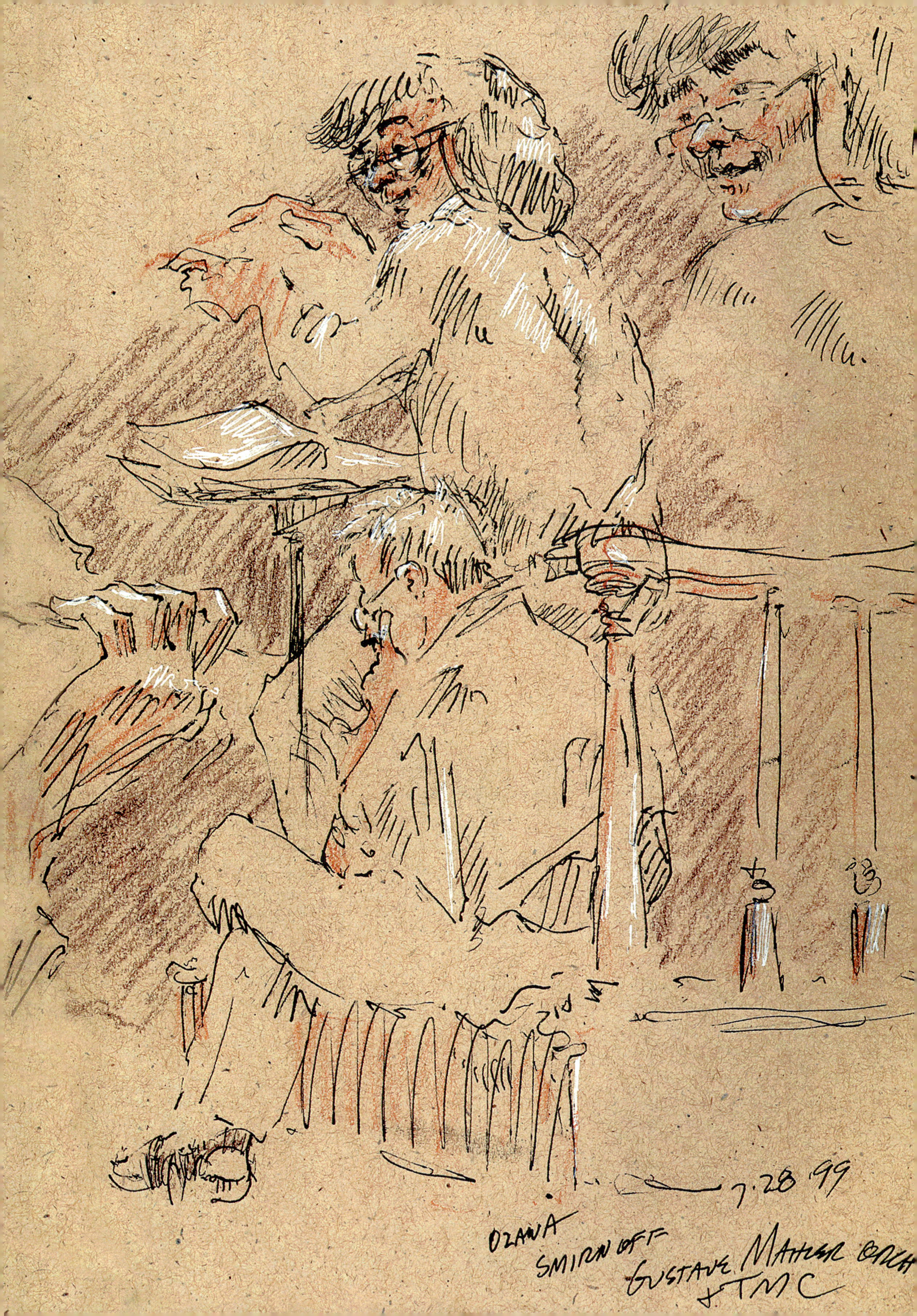
7.28.99
OZAWA
SMIRNOFF
GUSTAVE MAHLER ORCH
& TMC

I couldn't resist just a few more of these delicious Fellows.

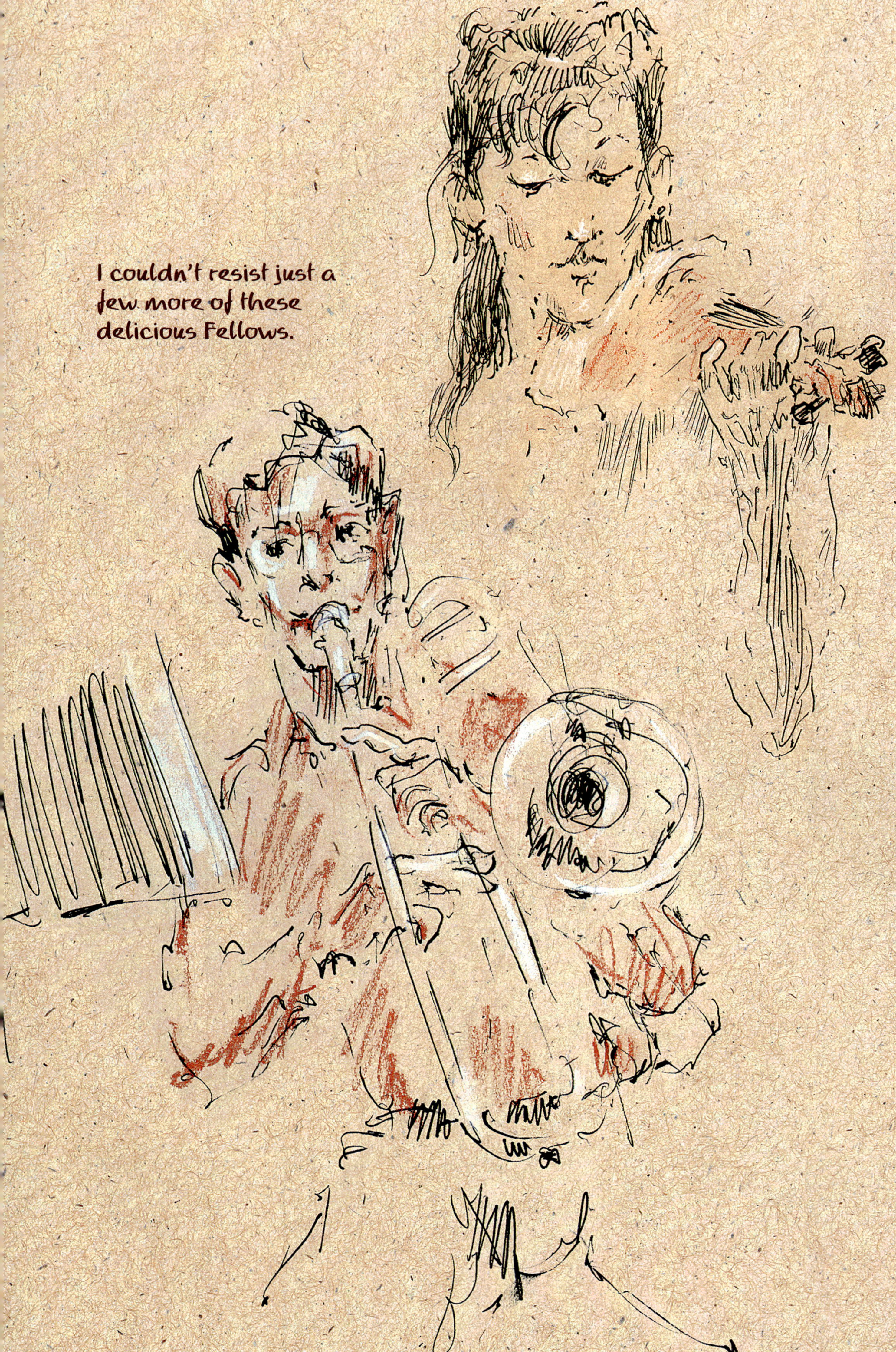

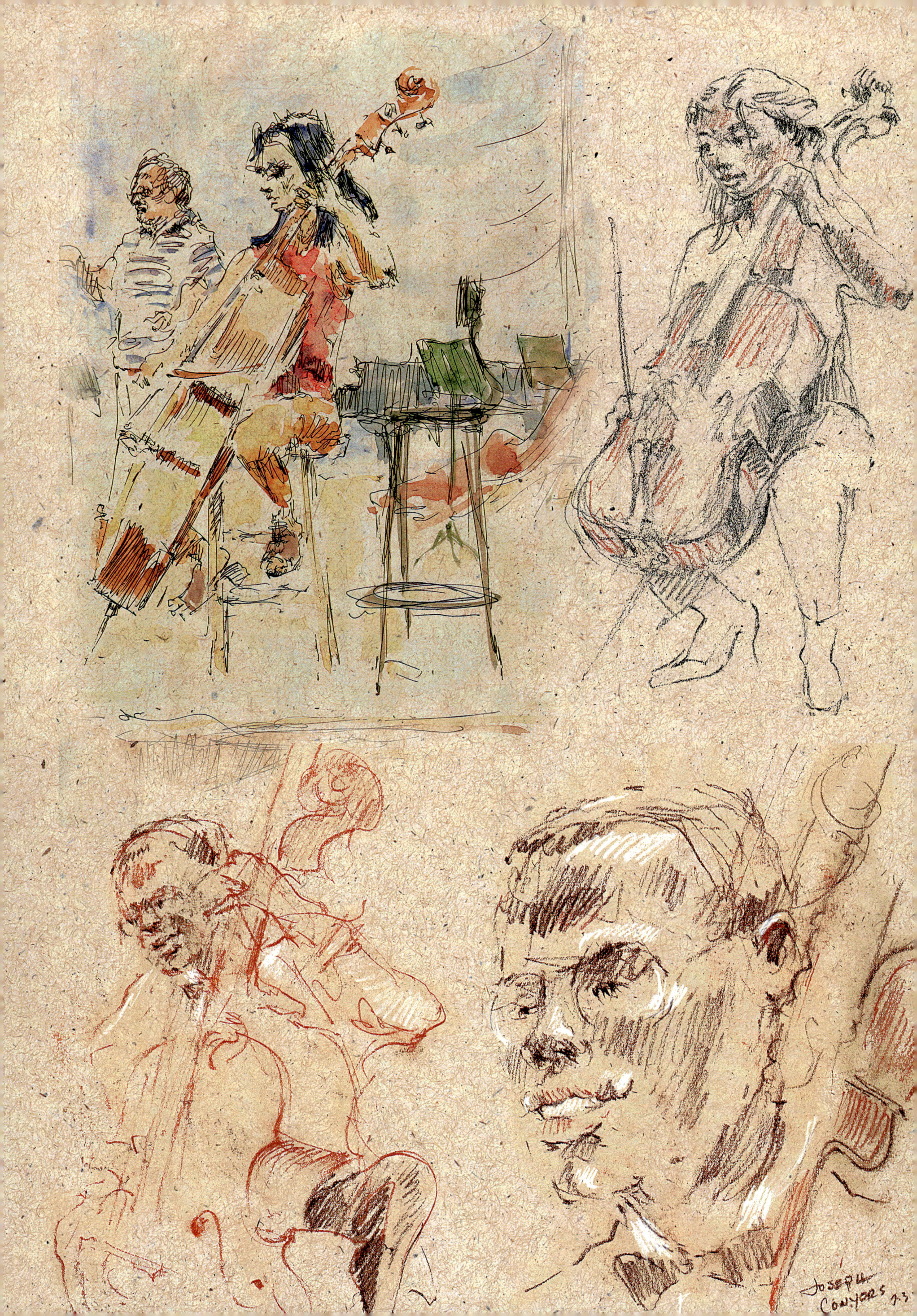
Joseph Conyers

Kalichstein Laredo, Robinson Trio

(Jaime Laredo, Jacob Kalichstein and Sharon Robinson)

When it comes to string trios, the greatest one since the original Beaux-Arts Trio disbanded (and keeps reconstituting itself), is the Kalichstein-Laredo-Robinson Trio.

Jaime Laredo, a great violinist and soloist, in the same rank as Itzhak Perlman and Pincus Zukerman, is the first violinist of this group. Jacob Kalichstein, a powerful yet wonderful ensemble player, is the pianist. And of course the beautiful Sharon Robinson, who plays and sounds like an orchestral cello section herself, is a very delicate, svelte, blond, young woman, yet the sound that emanates from that cello is absolutely spellbinding!

I drew them here in the Berkshires where all the great quartets perform. I showed them the drawings, and they were kind enough to autograph each one. Jaime wrote "thank you for this beautiful portrait," as did Jacob Kalichstein. Sharon wrote, "Dear Sol, thank you for capturing my soul."

There are three close-up portraits done with pen, and sepia, white and black conte pencil on Kraft paper, the same kind of paper used in paper bags.

There follows a drawing of the trio, full figure. They were doing the Schubert Opus 99 Piano Trio, one of the most beautiful ever written. I feel the drawing of the group caught the spirit of the moment and the inward look that each of them had as they played.

In the full figure drawing, Sharon is playing a passage where she is holding the bow in her hand and plucking the strings of the cello for a pizzicato sound, while Jaime is playing a beautiful solo passage. Notice, his right foot tends to twist back and forth on its heel, not so much to keep the beat but to deal with the intensity of the moment. You'll see that he has three feet in the drawing. Sometimes the feet of the performers are as interesting as their hands and faces.

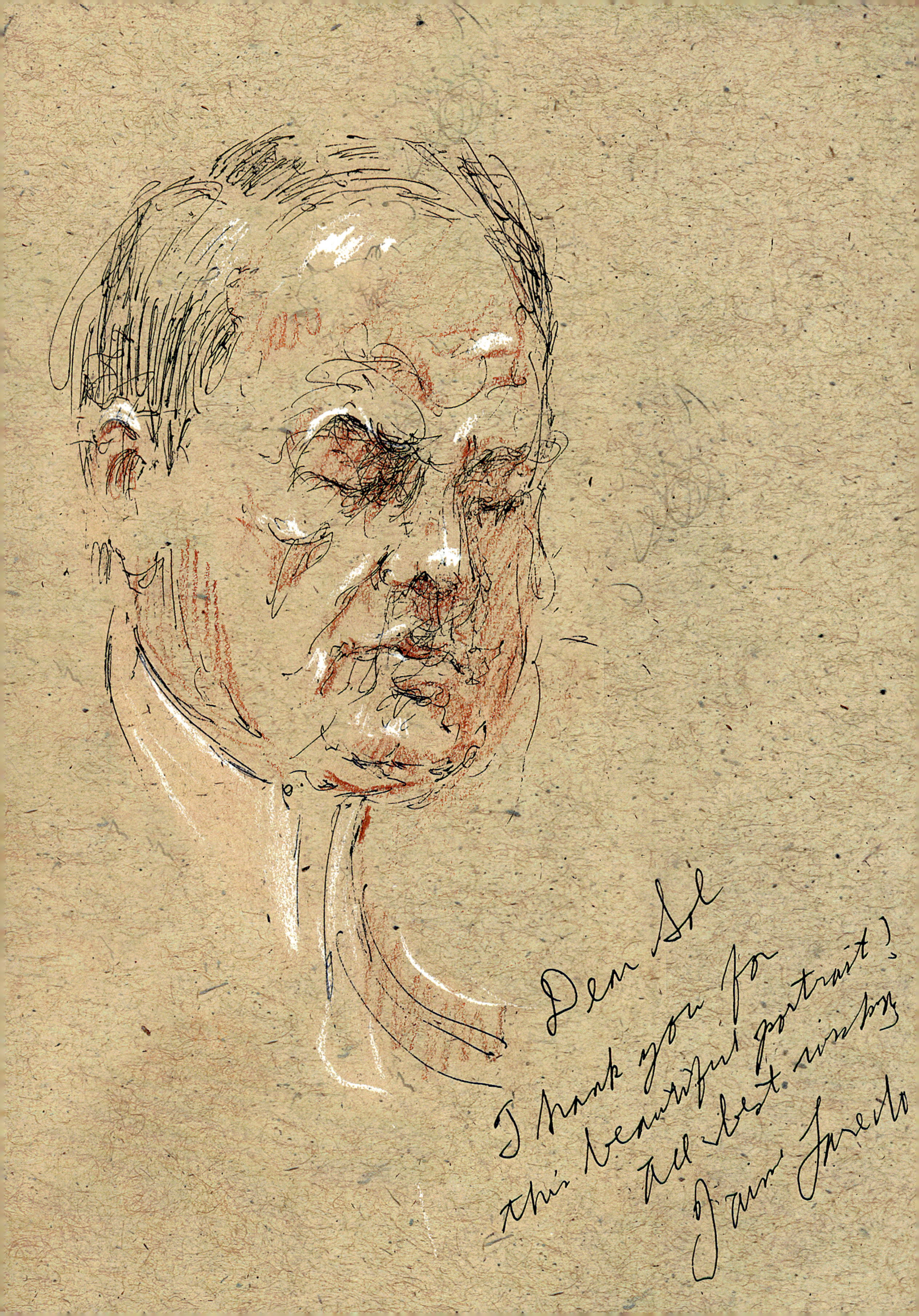
Dear Sol
Thank you for
this beautiful portrait!
All best wishes

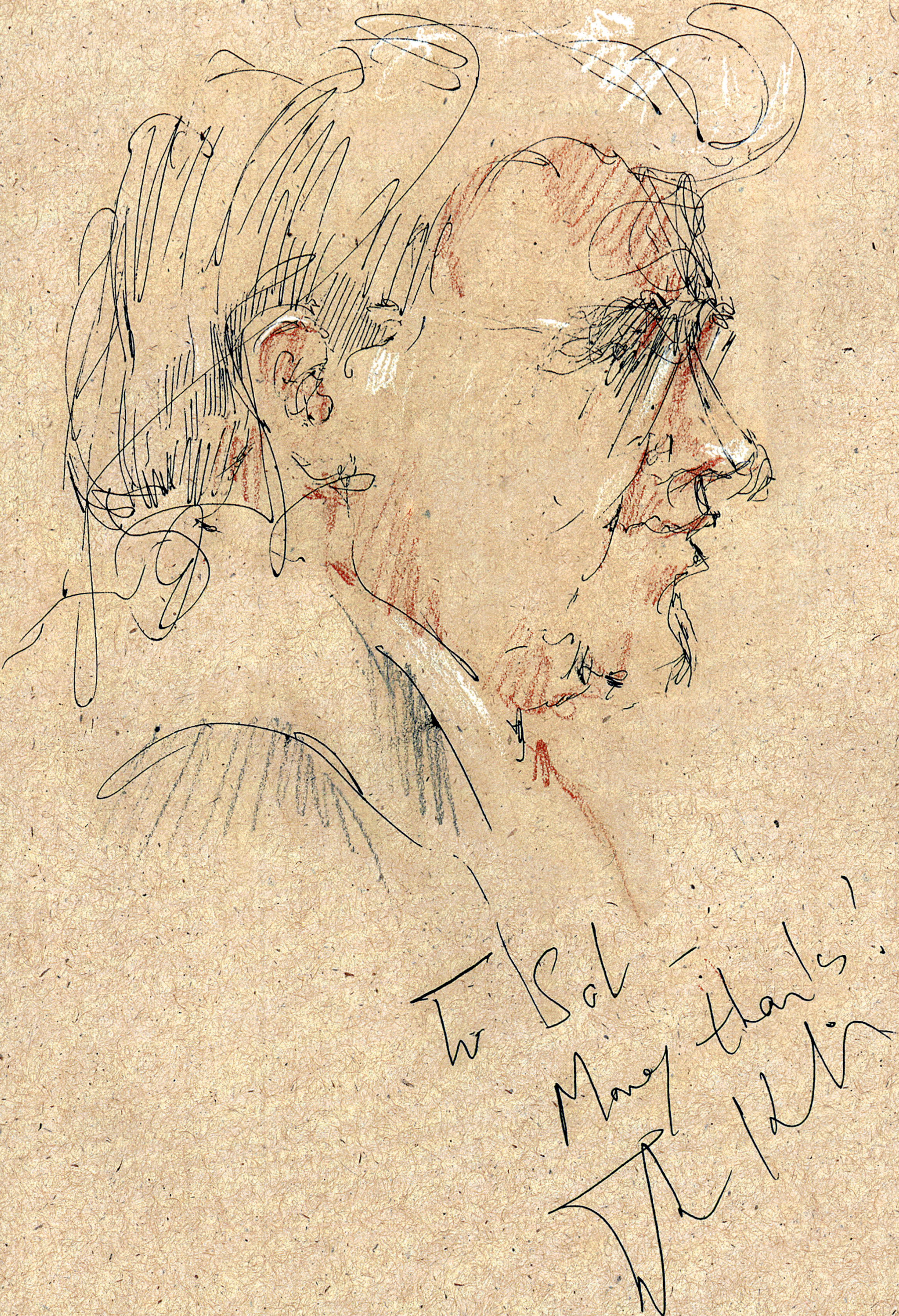
To Bob
Many thanks!

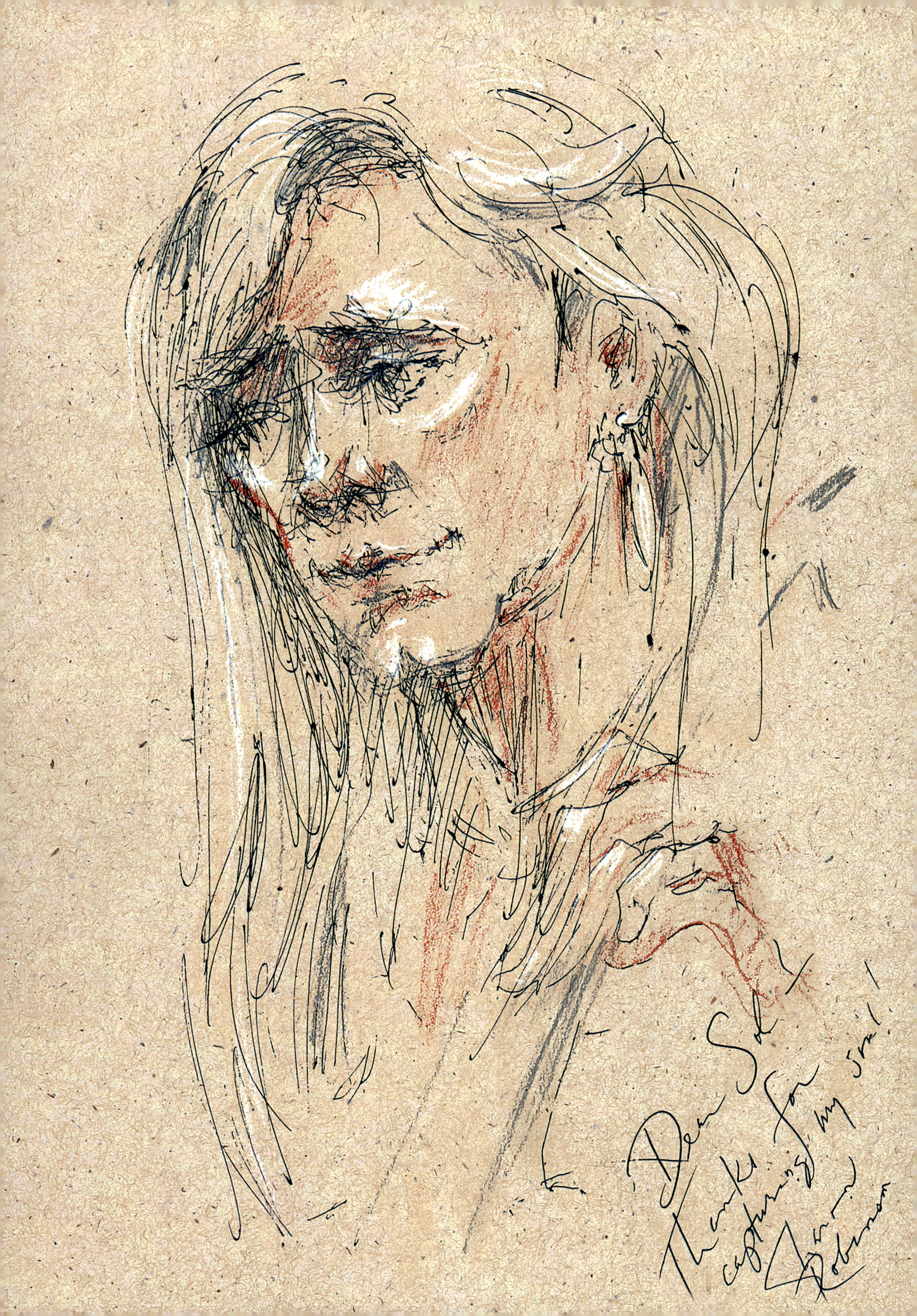
Dear Sol,
Thanks for capturing my soul!
Robinson

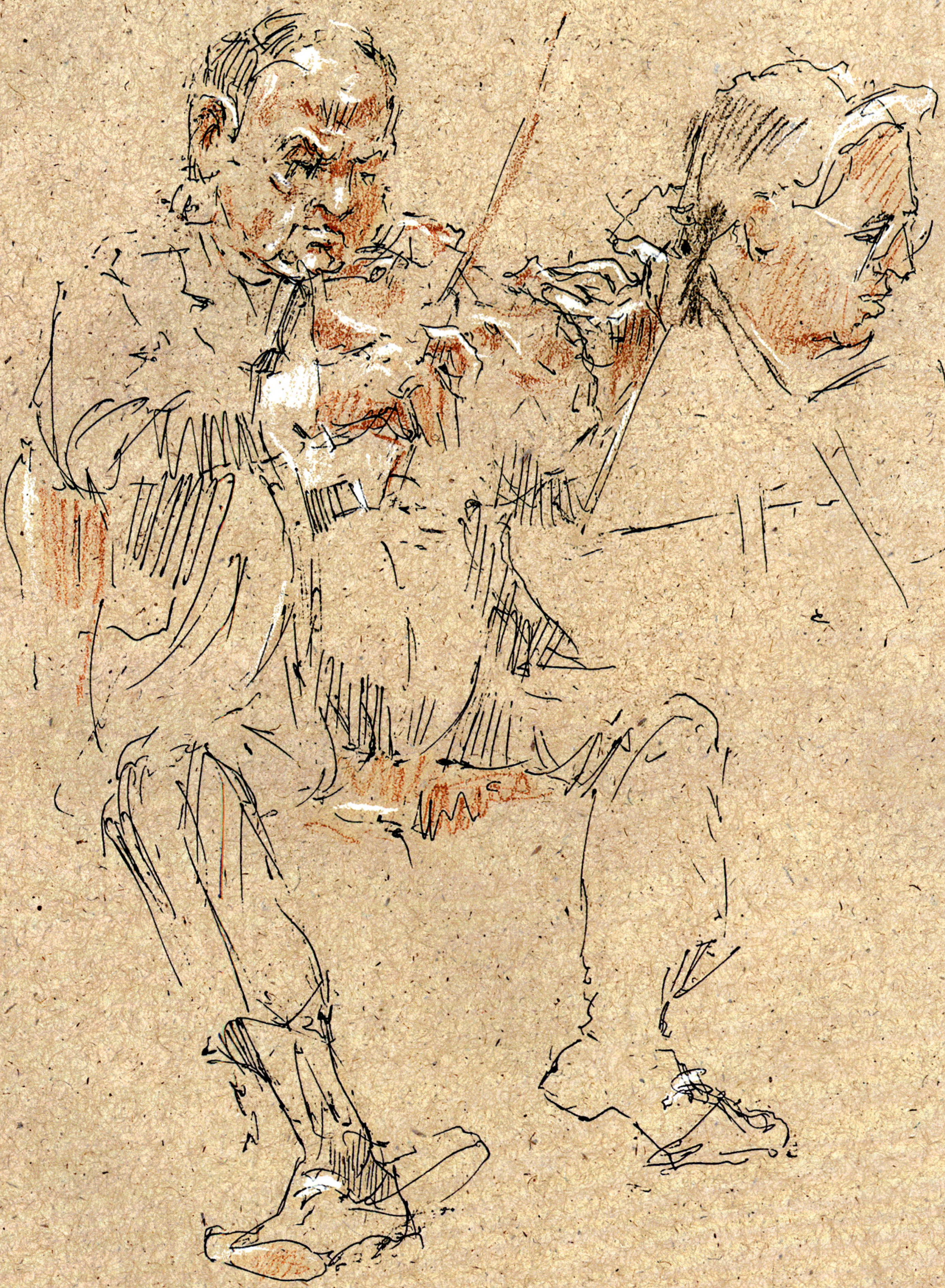

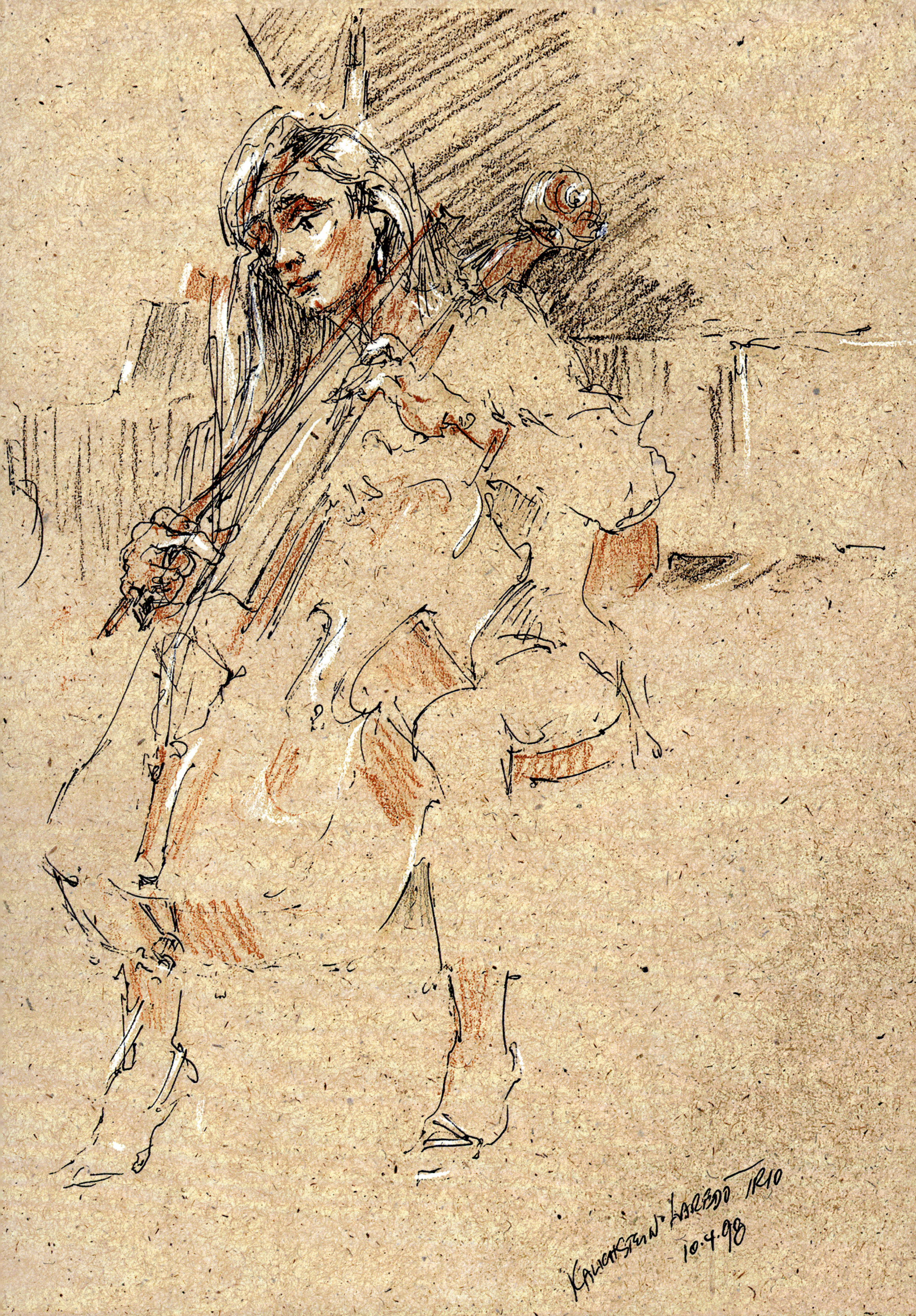
KALICHSTEIN-LAREDO TRIO
10.4.98

Yuri Bashmet and YoYo Ma

Yuri Bashmet, the great Russian violist, came to Ozawa hall to perform a sonata with his daughter and play the Schumann quartet with Emanuel Ax, Malcolm Lowe and YoYo Ma. The place was packed. There was a huge audience out on the lawn. Every seat in Ozawa hall was taken. I sat on the stage so my view of Bashmet was his back, as you can see in this brush drawing I did.

There was a huge thunderstorm, a great number of the outdoor audience had to crowd at the entrance of Ozawa hall. Lightning and thunder crashed while they were doing the Schumann quartet. A great deal of the sound was obliterated. At the end of the quartet the lights went out almost simultaneously with the last note. Bashmet, who is a smoker, had a flame-thrower cigarette lighter. He lit the group on the stage as they took their bows to a completely blacked-out auditorium. The audience would not let them go; they kept calling them back, stamping their feet and applauding. It was, when you could hear it, a beautiful performance.

Suddenly the lights went on again and Emanuel Ax announced that they would perform the third movement again and this time, "he hoped they would hear it." Someone from the second row, center, left in a rush to get home. I left the stage and took that seat and got Bashmet full face from the front. His figure, face and dynamism make me think that this is what Paganini must have been like. I also caught Emanuel Ax, Malcolm Lowe and YoYo Ma. It was a very exciting and wonderful performance and quite an unusual event.

I must note that some of the problems of drawing musicians are that they are very animated and move around a lot. Those few that remain still are easier to catch. YoYo Ma is not one of the latter. He is so mercurial and animated and almost never stops moving while playing. How he does this is a wonder to everyone since he will either wrap himself around the cello, look very serious, scrunch his eyes so that he looks like he's crying or lean back and laugh. And so, he's not easy to do.

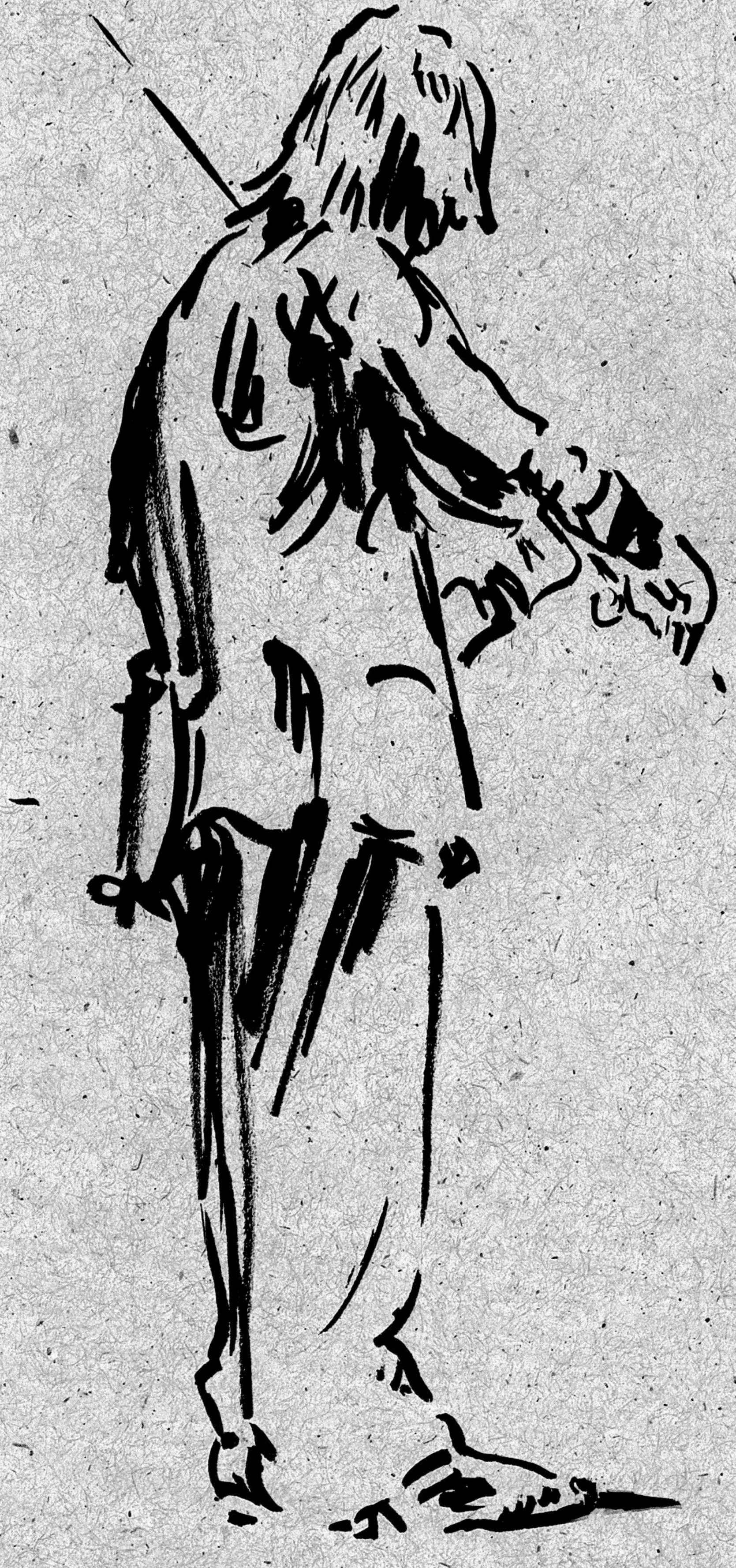

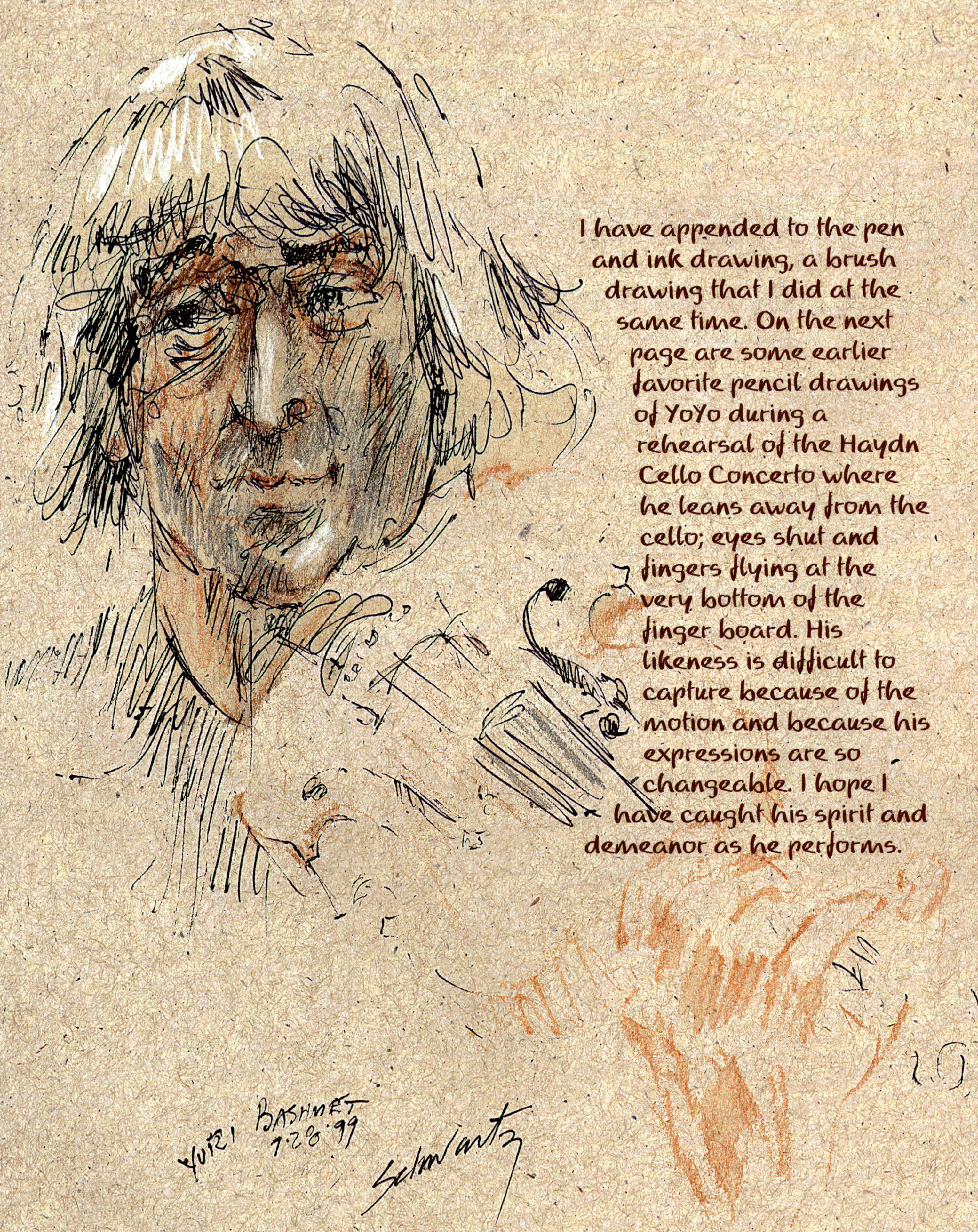

I have appended to the pen and ink drawing, a brush drawing that I did at the same time. On the next page are some earlier favorite pencil drawings of YoYo during a rehearsal of the Haydn Cello Concerto where he leans away from the cello; eyes shut and fingers flying at the very bottom of the finger board. His likeness is difficult to capture because of the motion and because his expressions are so changeable. I hope I have caught his spirit and demeanor as he performs.

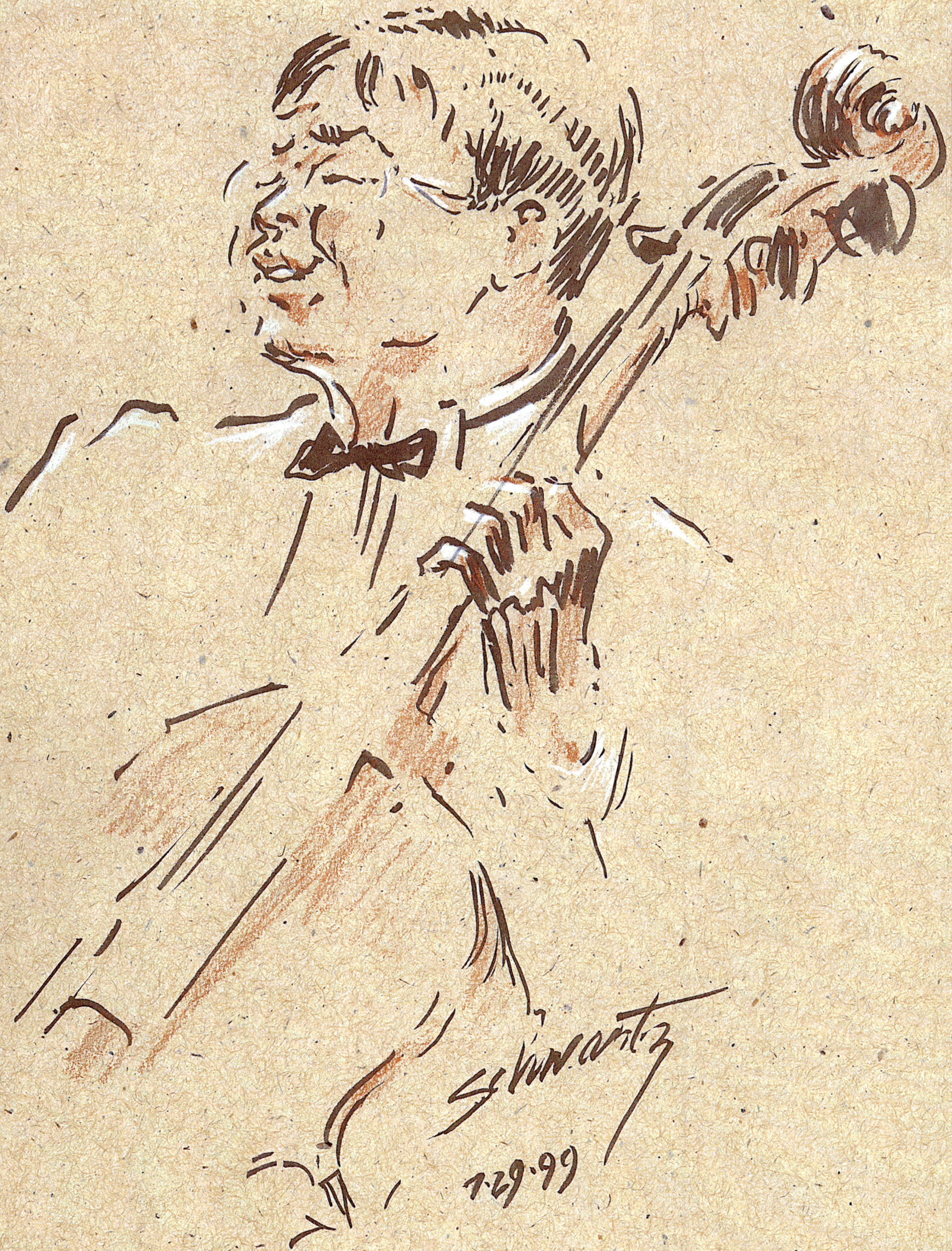
Schwartz
7·29·99

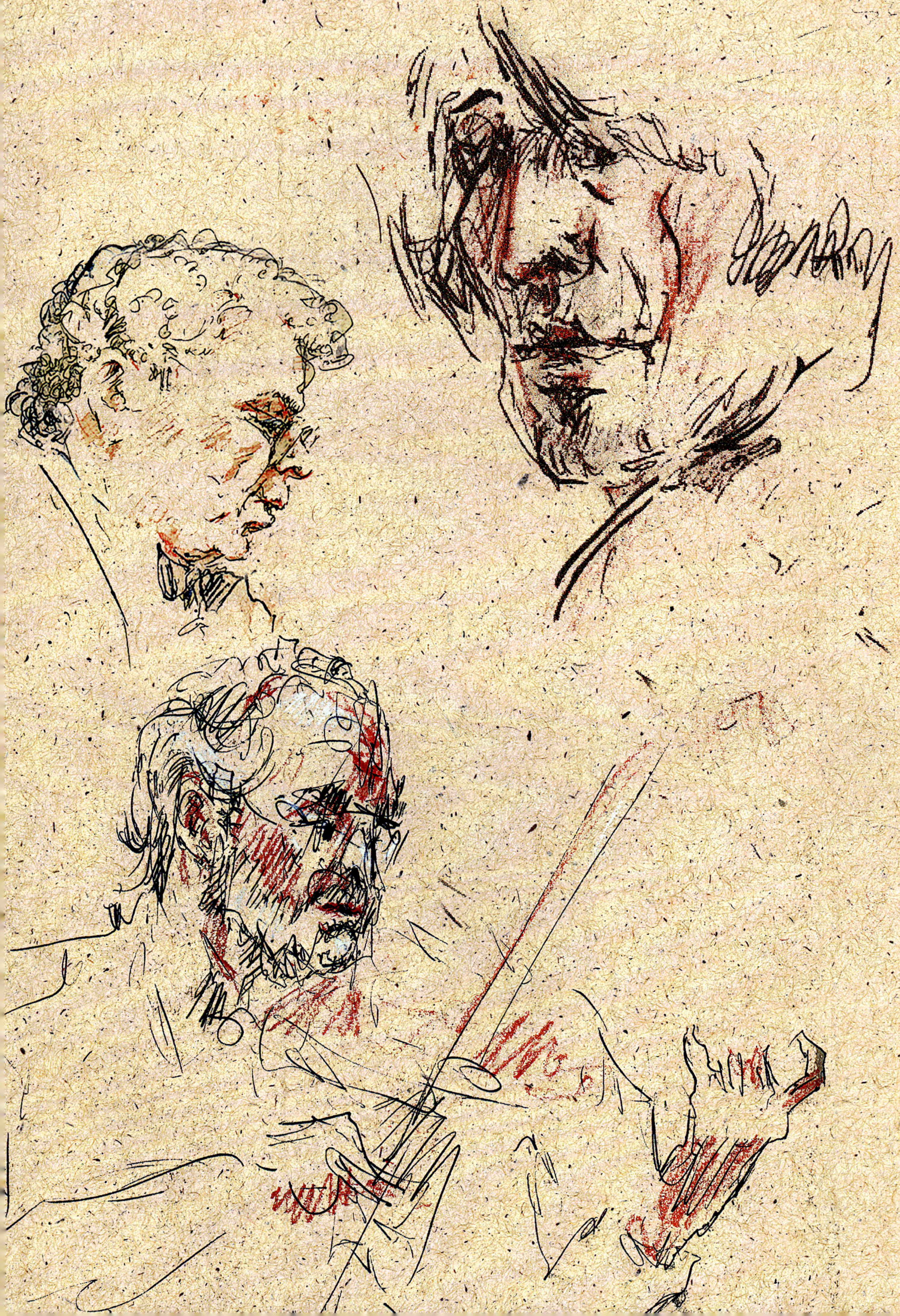

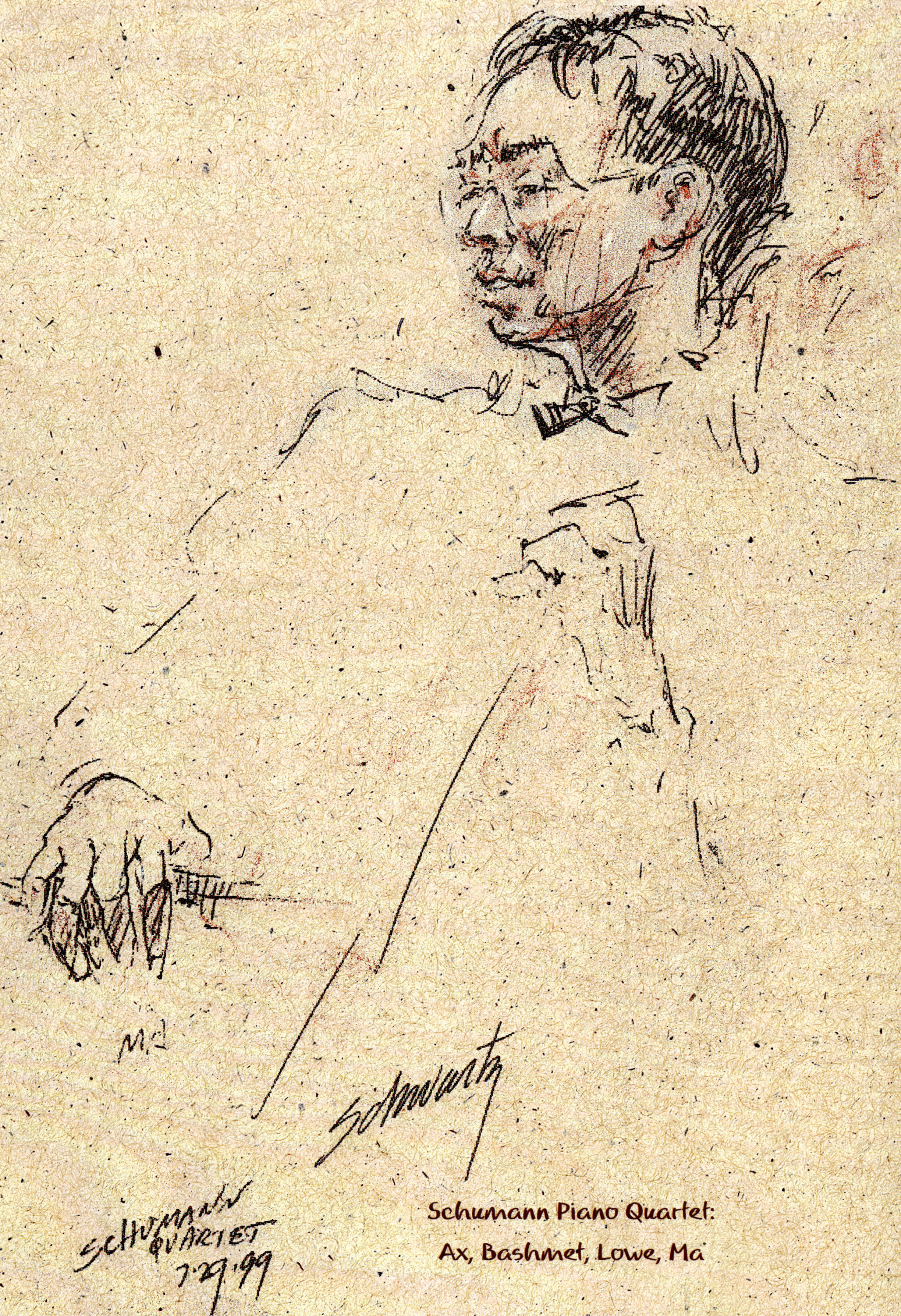

Schumann Piano Quartet:
Ax, Bashmet, Lowe, Ma

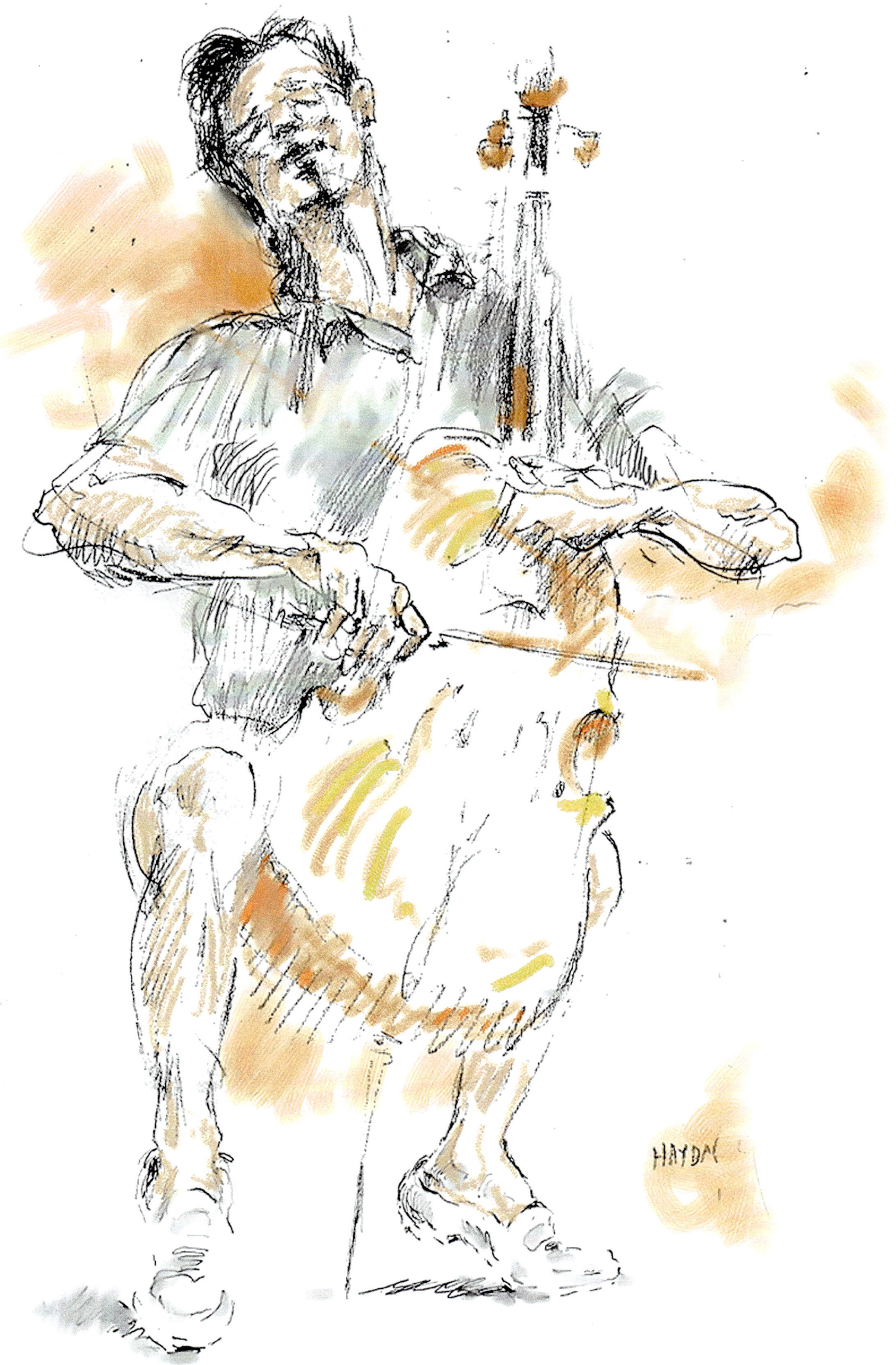
HAYDN

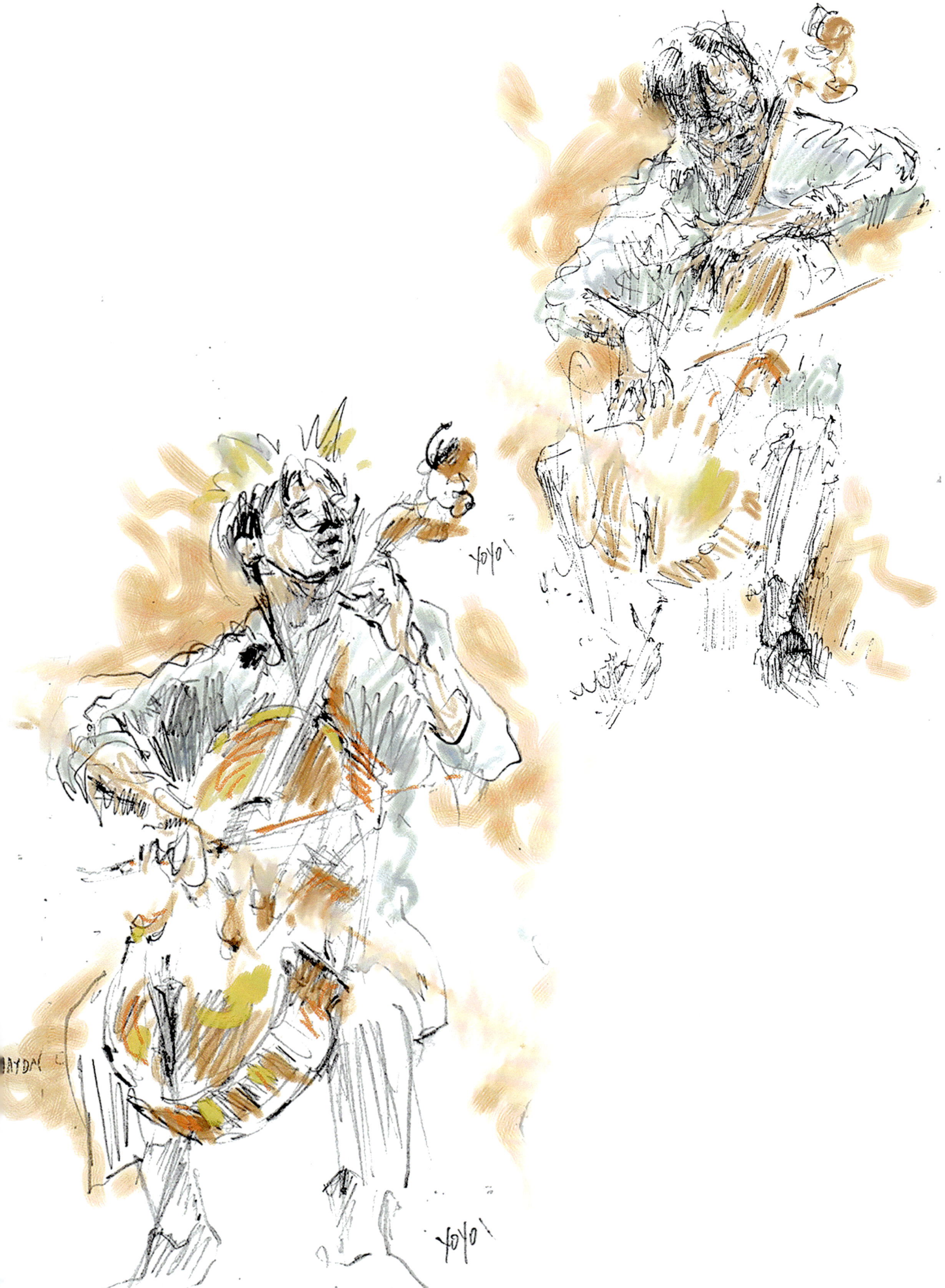
YOYO!
YOYO!

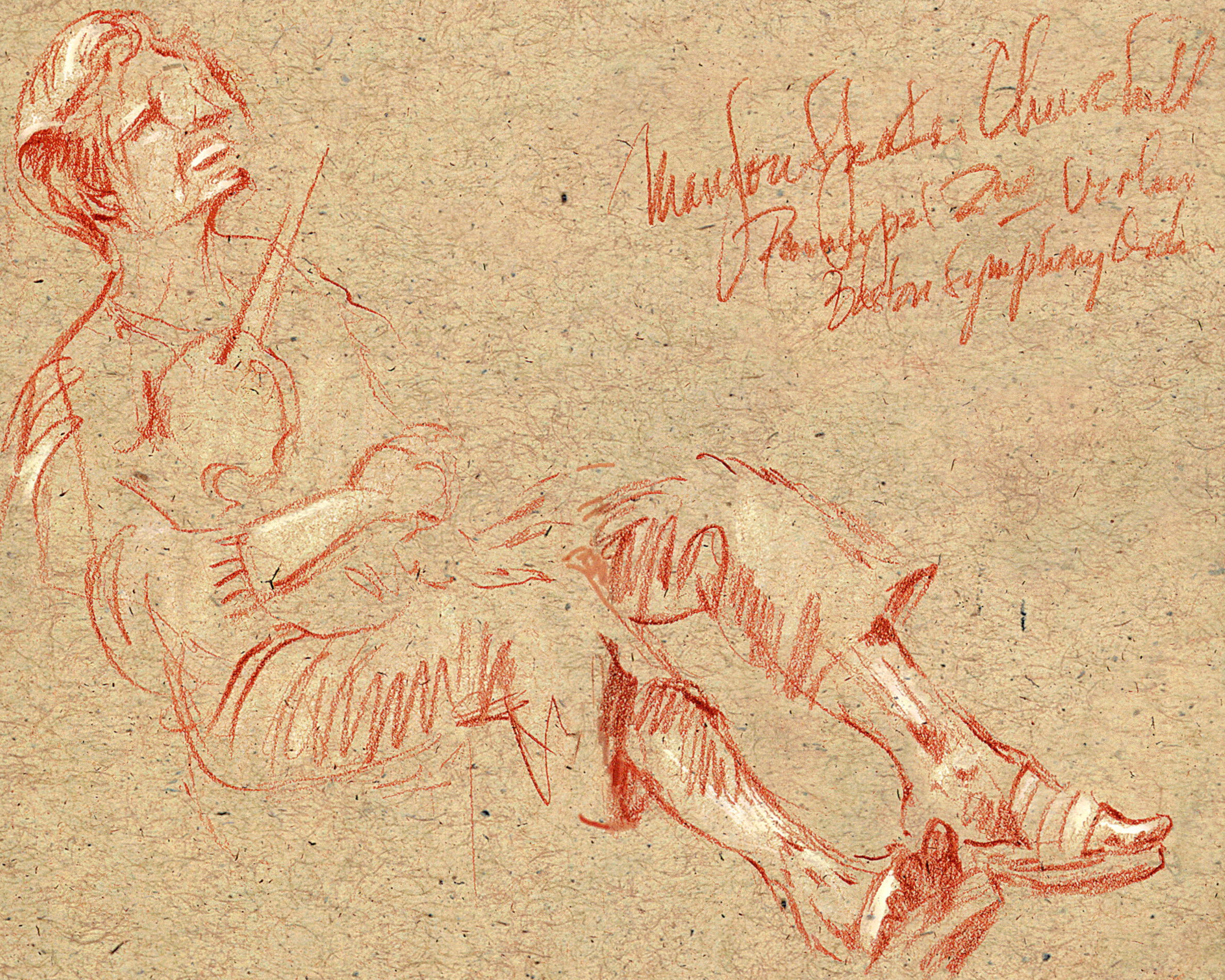

The Boston Symphony Orchestra & Seiji Ozawa

During a Saturday open rehearsal, Seiji Ozawa forgot his glasses. Marylou Speaker Churchill principal second violin sits next to the podium. She is tall and even with a raised podium can look down at the conductor's score and give him the measure numbers he could not see without glasses.

So, up and down she went saying the measure number loud and clear and the Maestro repeating it to the orchestra each time. Soon everyone was laughing, especially Ms. Churchill, who you can see rocking back in her seat as she sat once again. This time with her toes up in the air.

She enjoyed the drawing and autographed it.

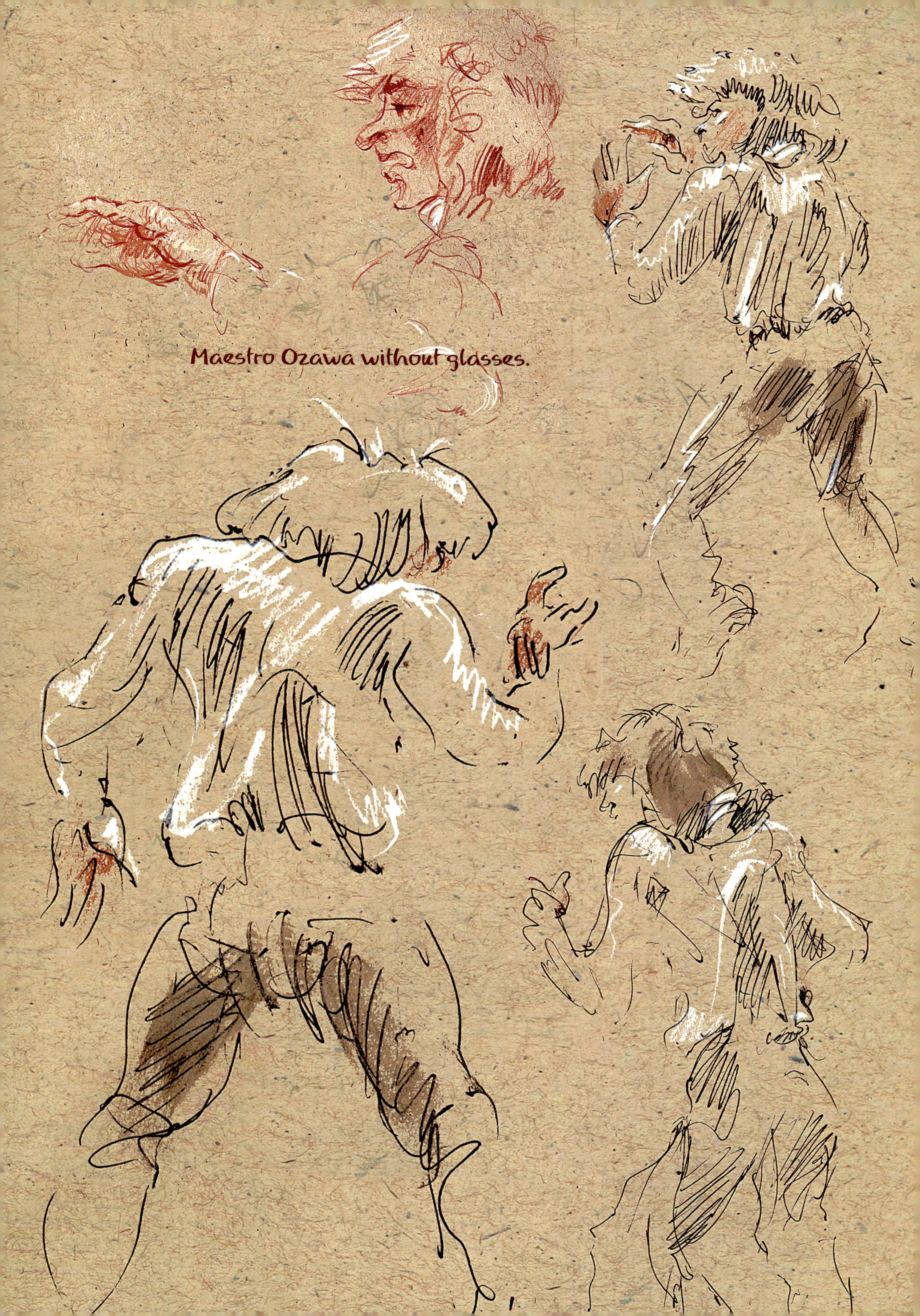

Maestro Ozawa without glasses.

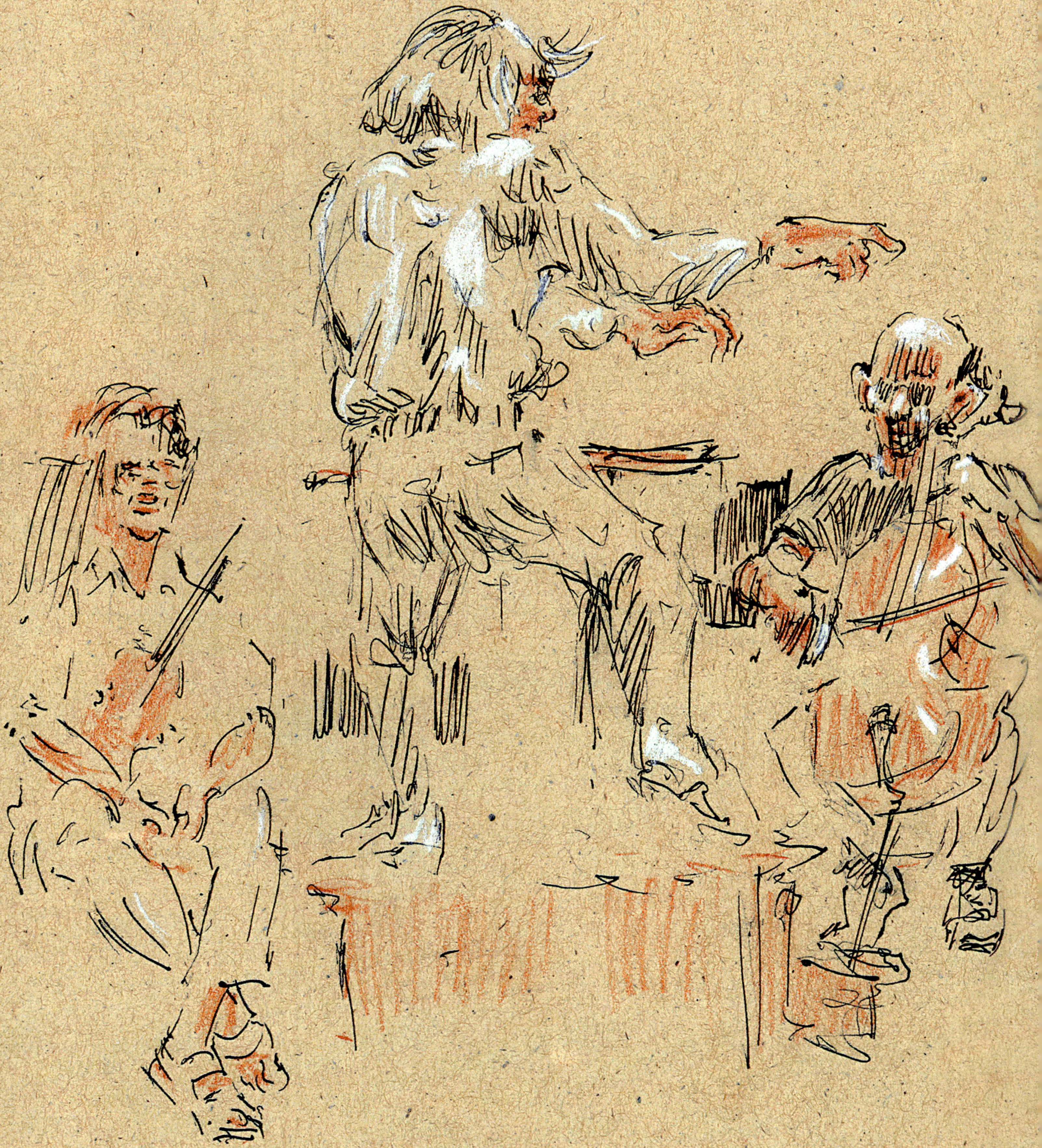

Seiji Ozawa and the BSO in rehearsal

You may be able to recognize these rapid sketches of Marylou Speaker Churchill, violin, Jules Eskind, cello, Burton Fine, viola and Michael Zaretsky, viola.

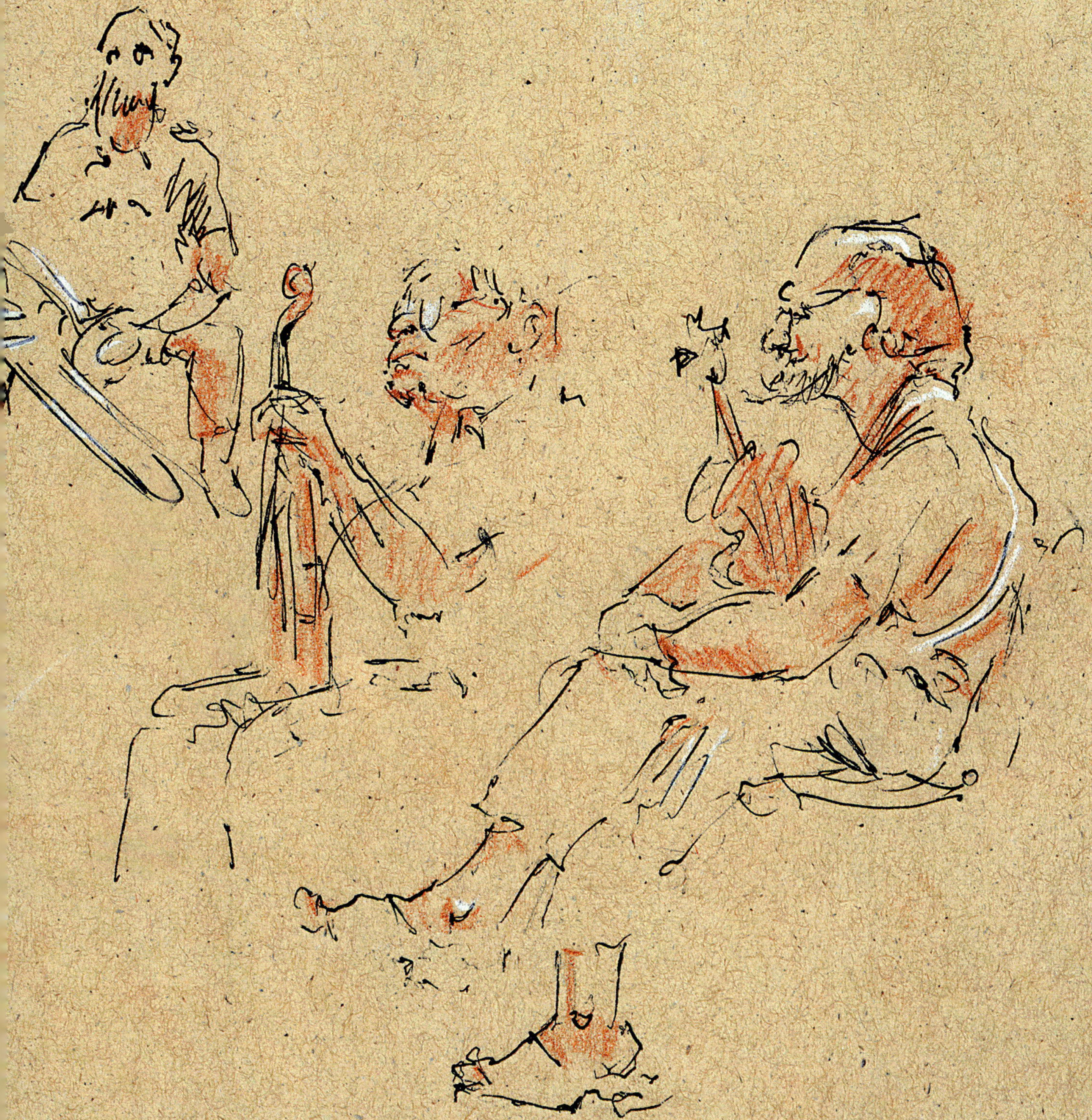

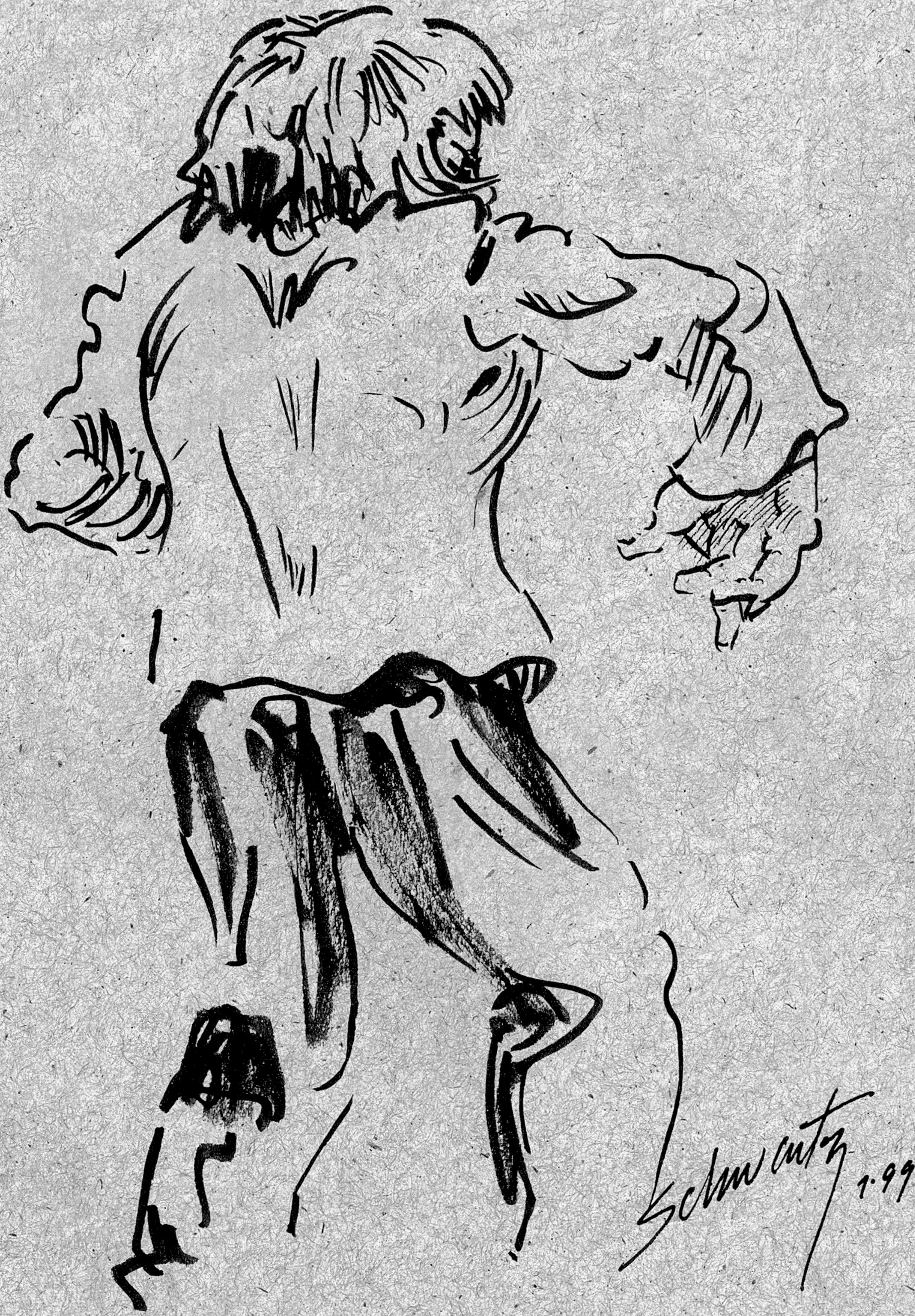
Schwartz
1·99

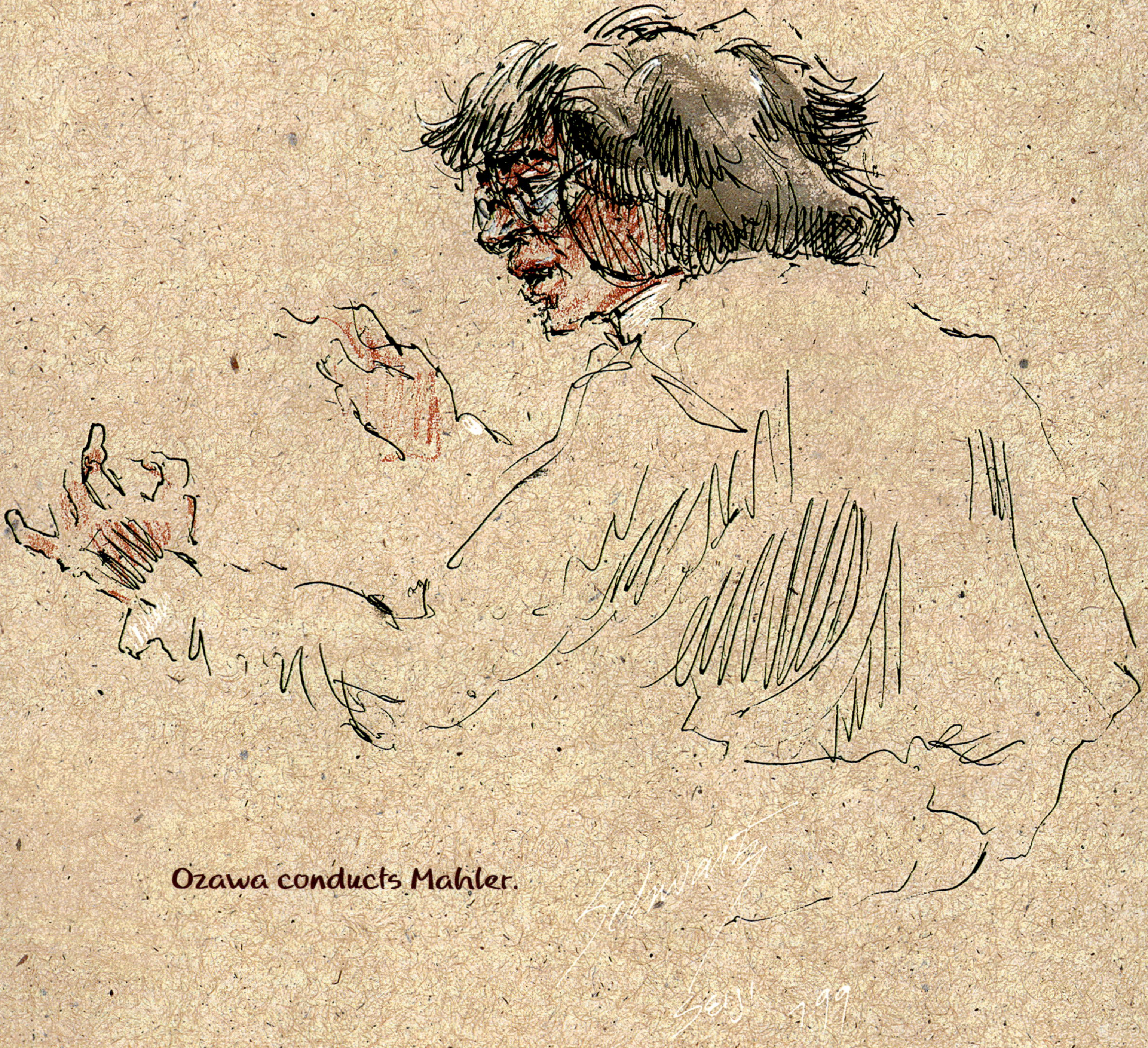

Ozawa conducts Mahler.

Maestro Ozawa conducts the opening concert of the TMC season (left)

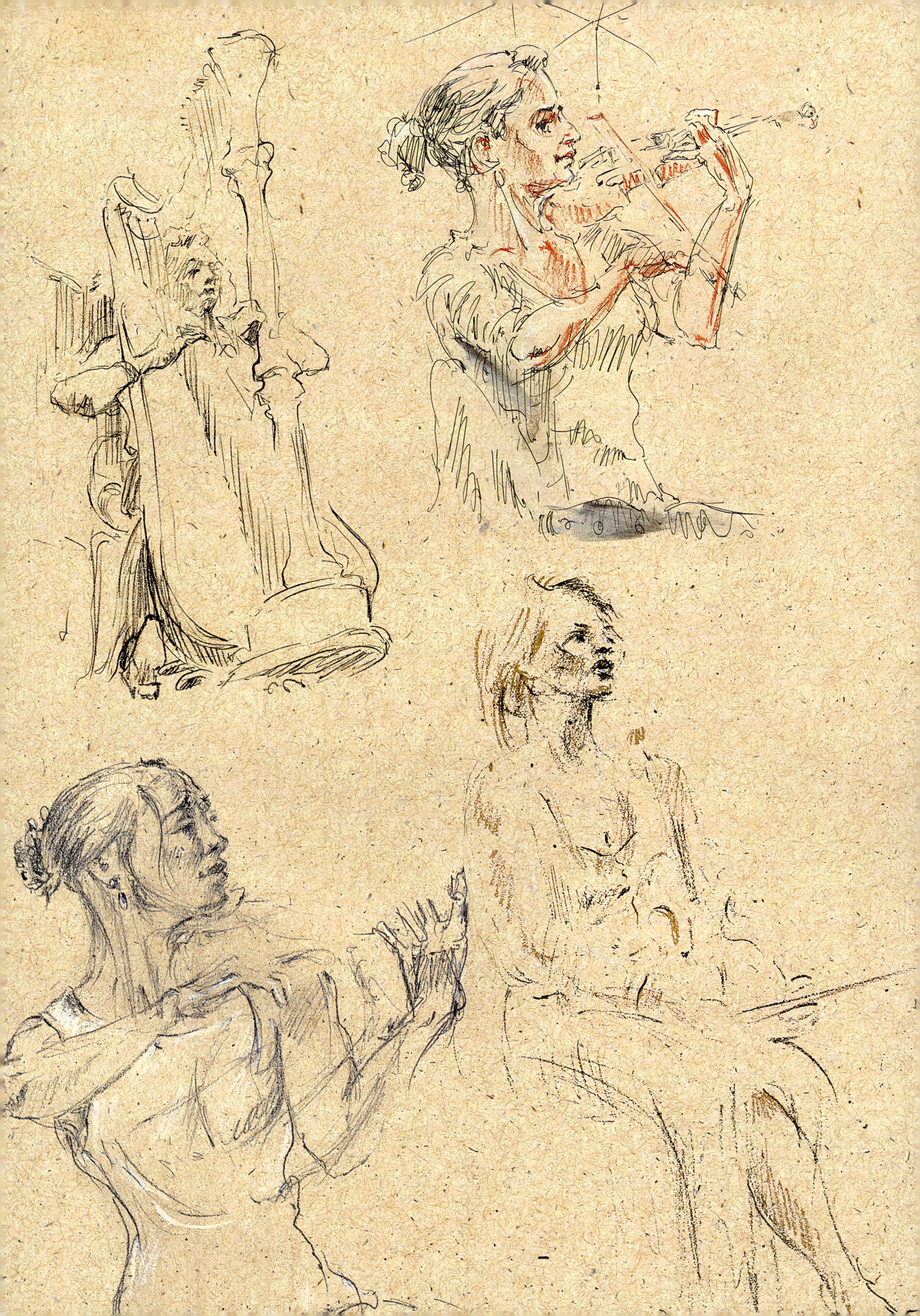

BSO members

Each a soloist in their own right, makes this one of the world's great orchestras.

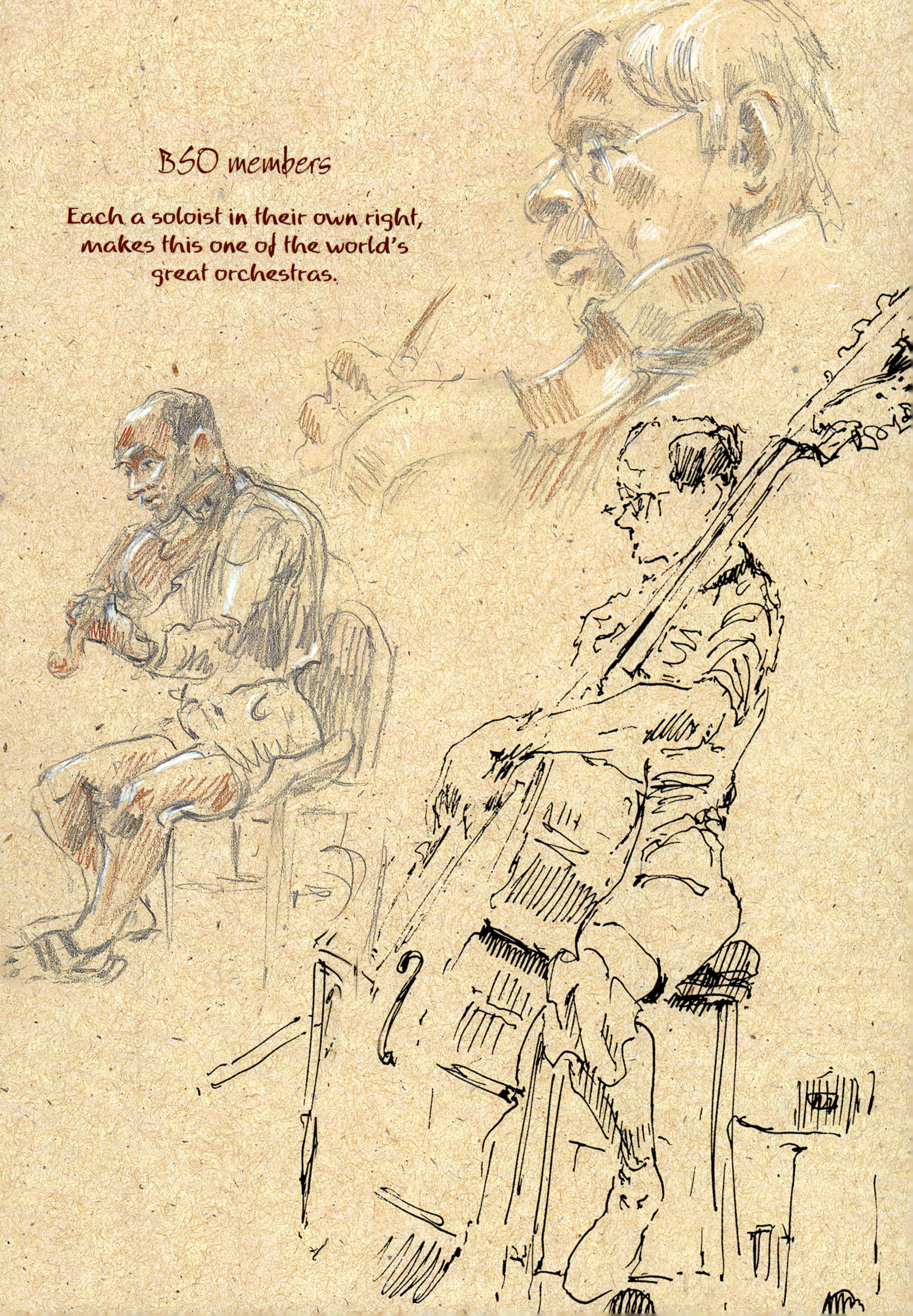

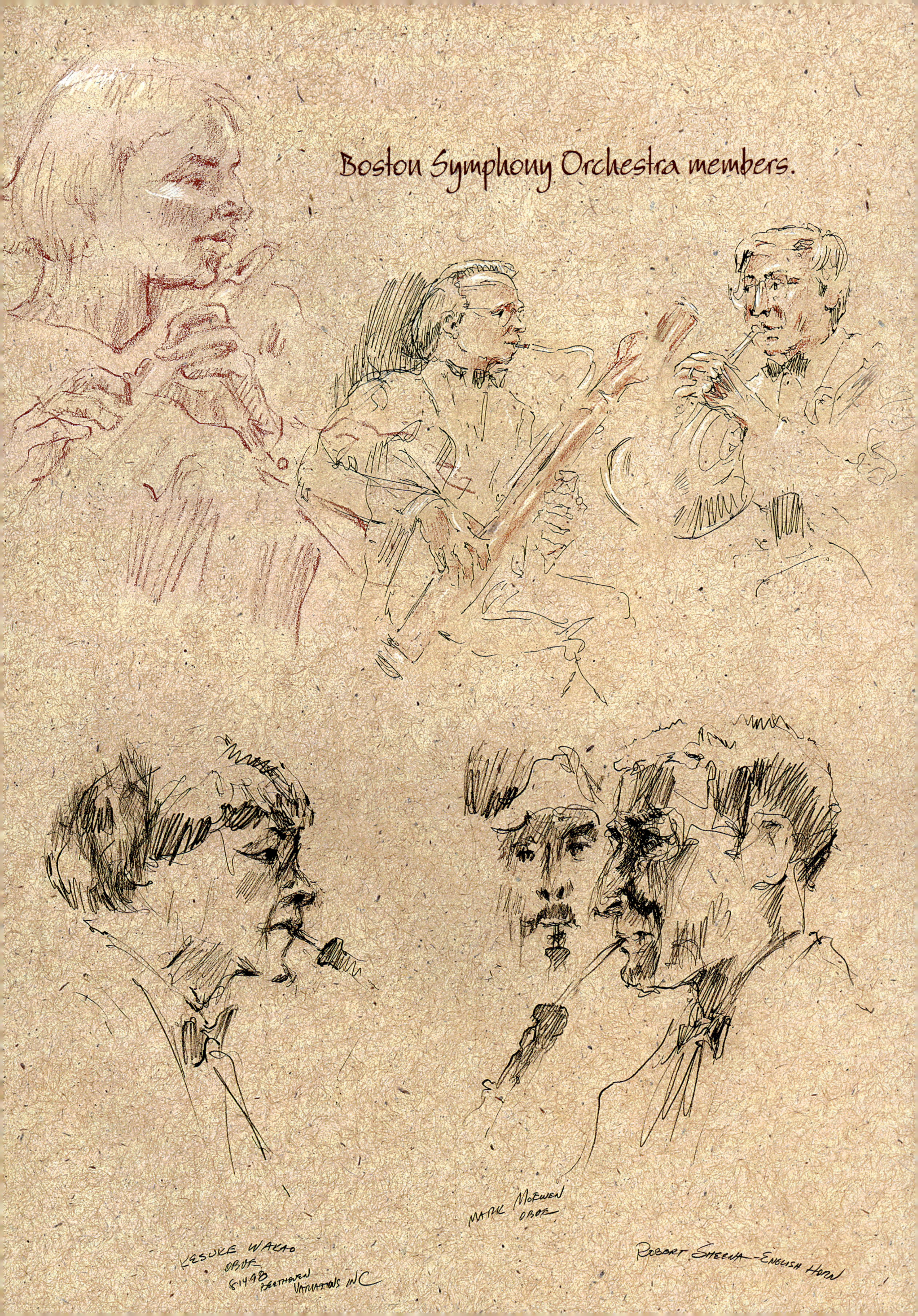
Boston Symphony Orchestra members.
KESUKE WAKAO
OBOE
6.14.98 BEETHOVEN VARIATIONS IN C
MARK McEWEN
OBOE
ROBERT SHEENA — ENGLISH HORN

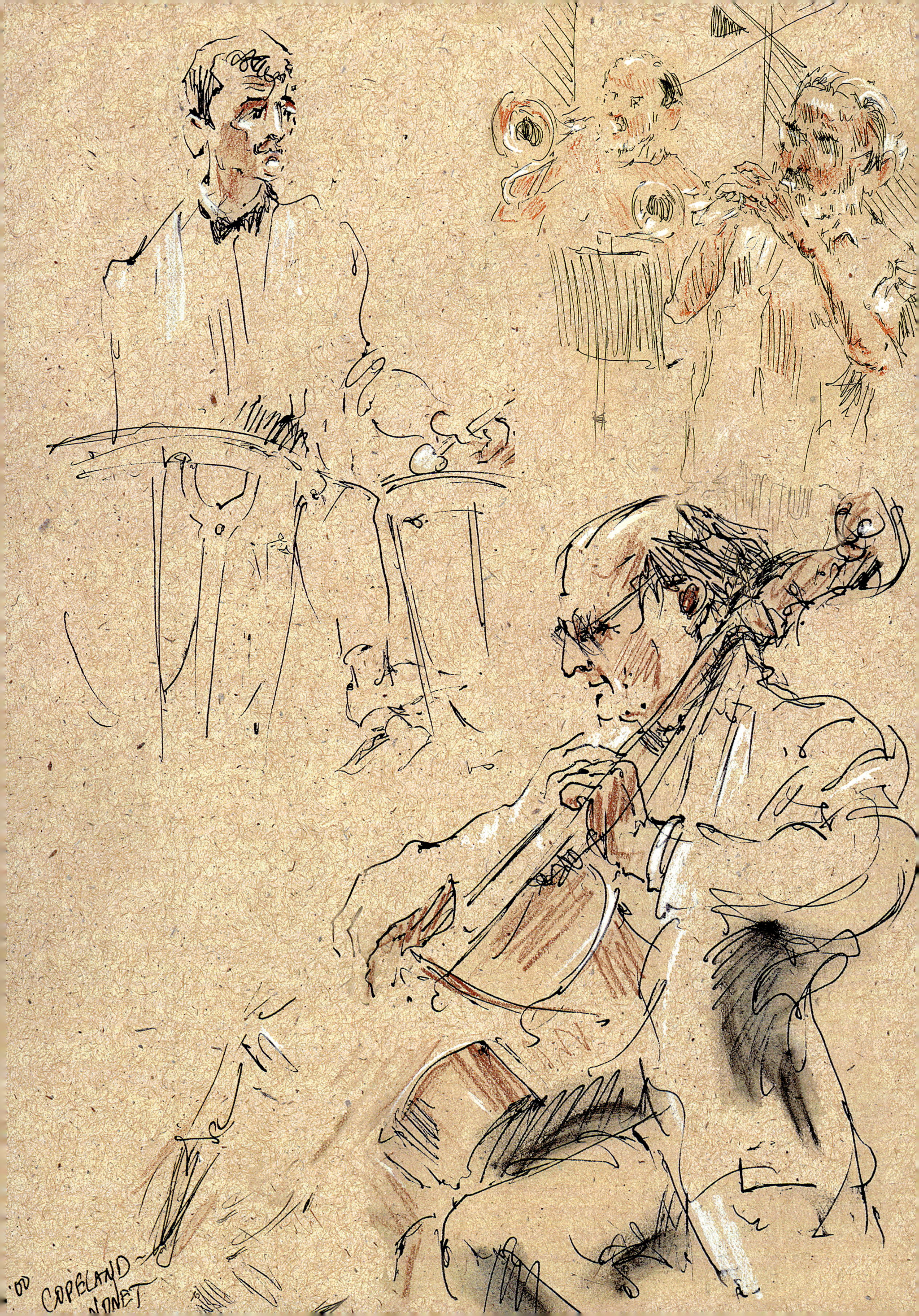
'00
COPELAND
NONET

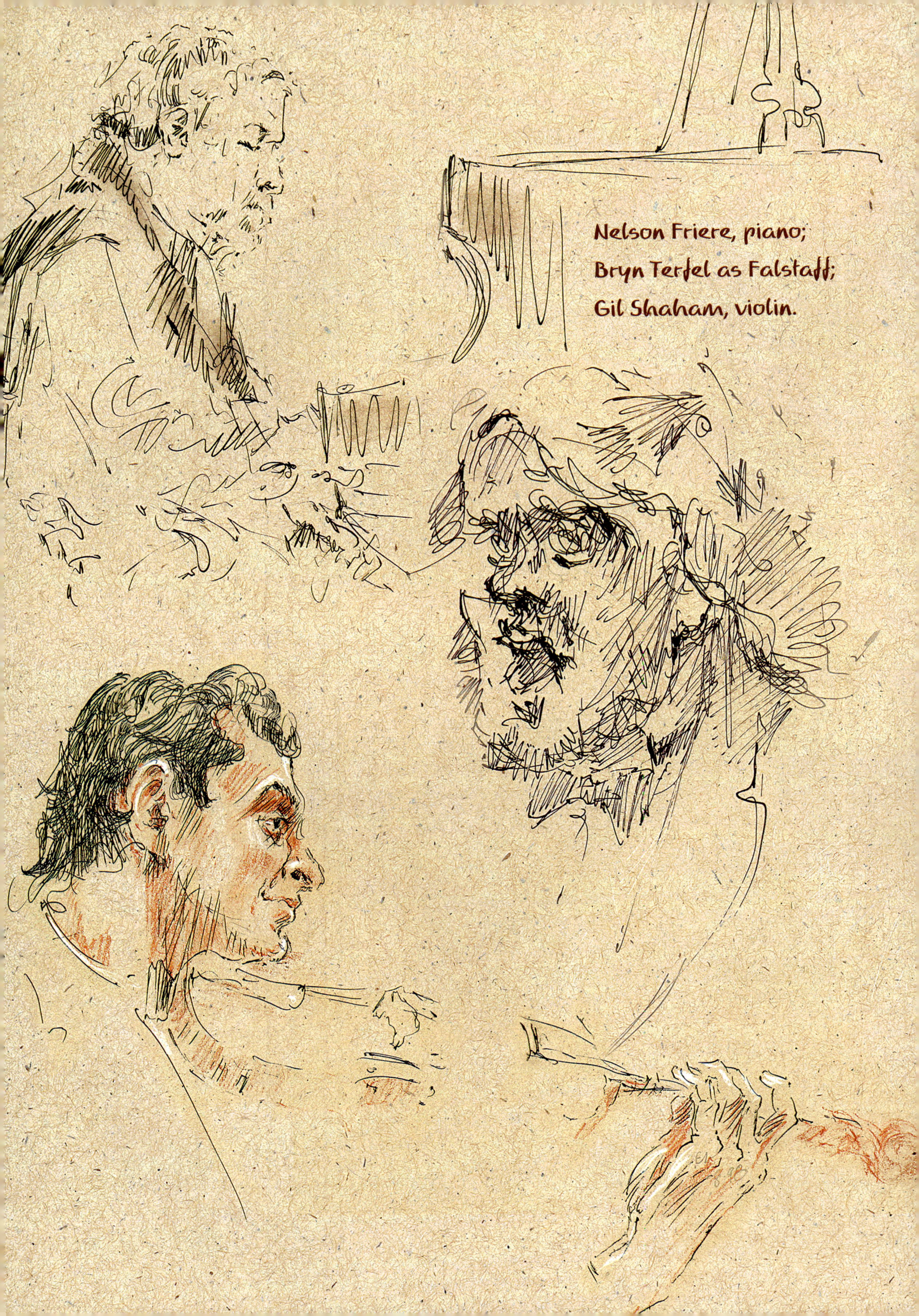

Nelson Friere, piano;
Bryn Terfel as Falstaff;
Gil Shaham, violin.

Tanglewood Guest Artists

The most distinguished performers, conductors and chamber groups join the BSO each summer both in the Tanglewood shed and in Ozawa Hall. Here is a very brief selection that will be enlarged in another volume of Drawing Music.

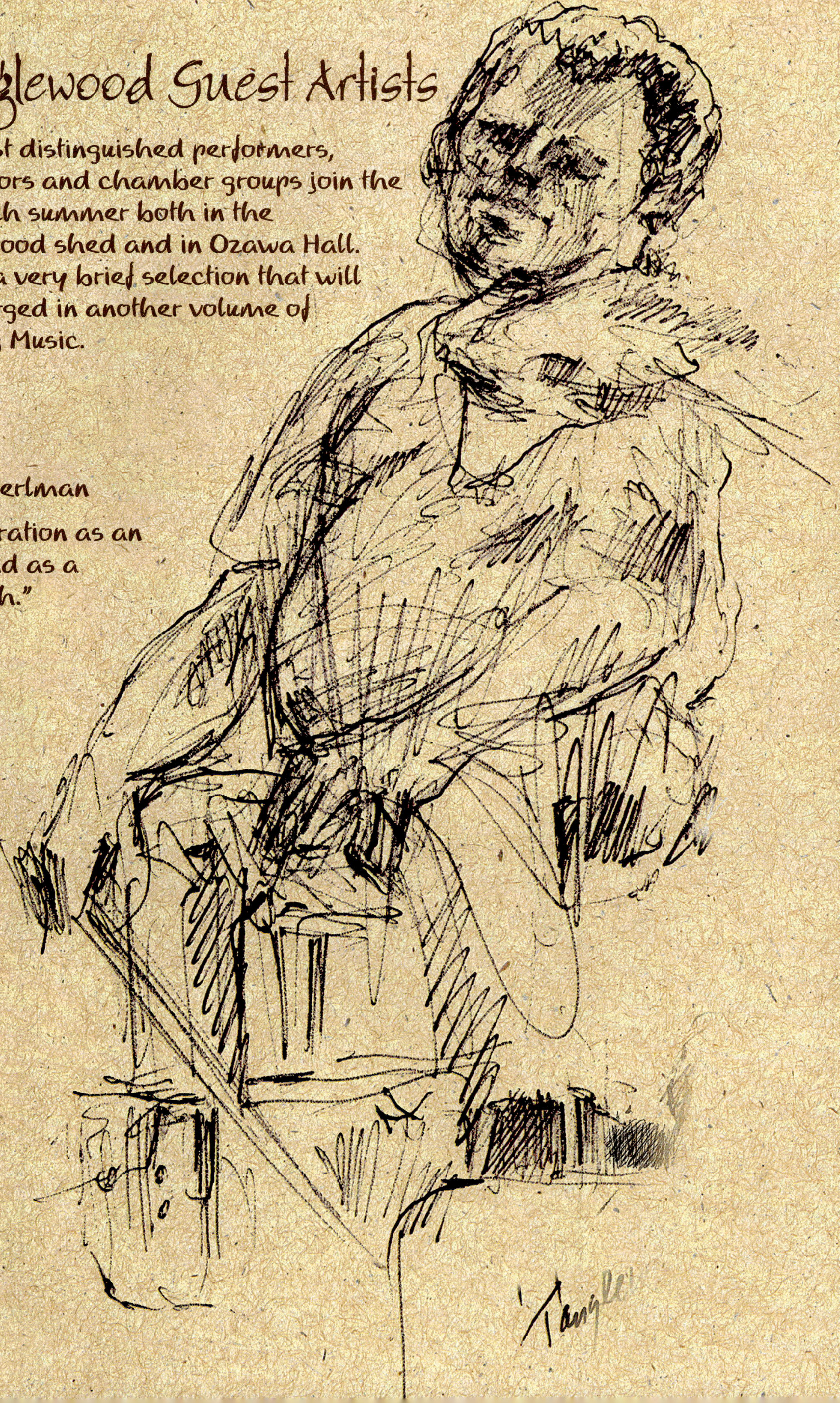

Itzhak Perlman

An inspiration as an artist and as a "Mentsch."

Tanglewood Guest Artists

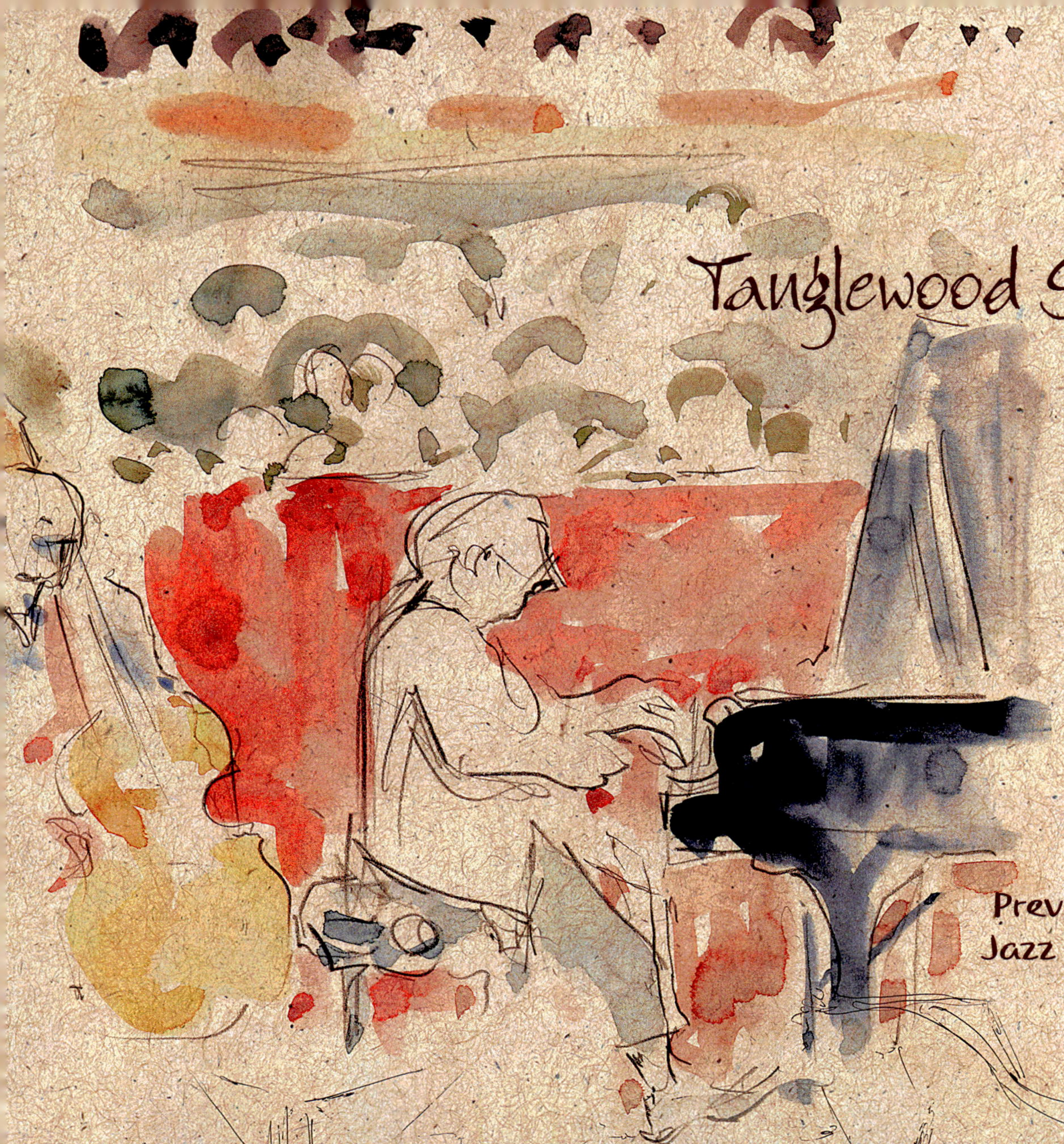

Previn and Finck do Jazz at Ozawa Hall.

Steven Hough hangs his jacket on the piano as he rehearses the Mozart 24th concerto.

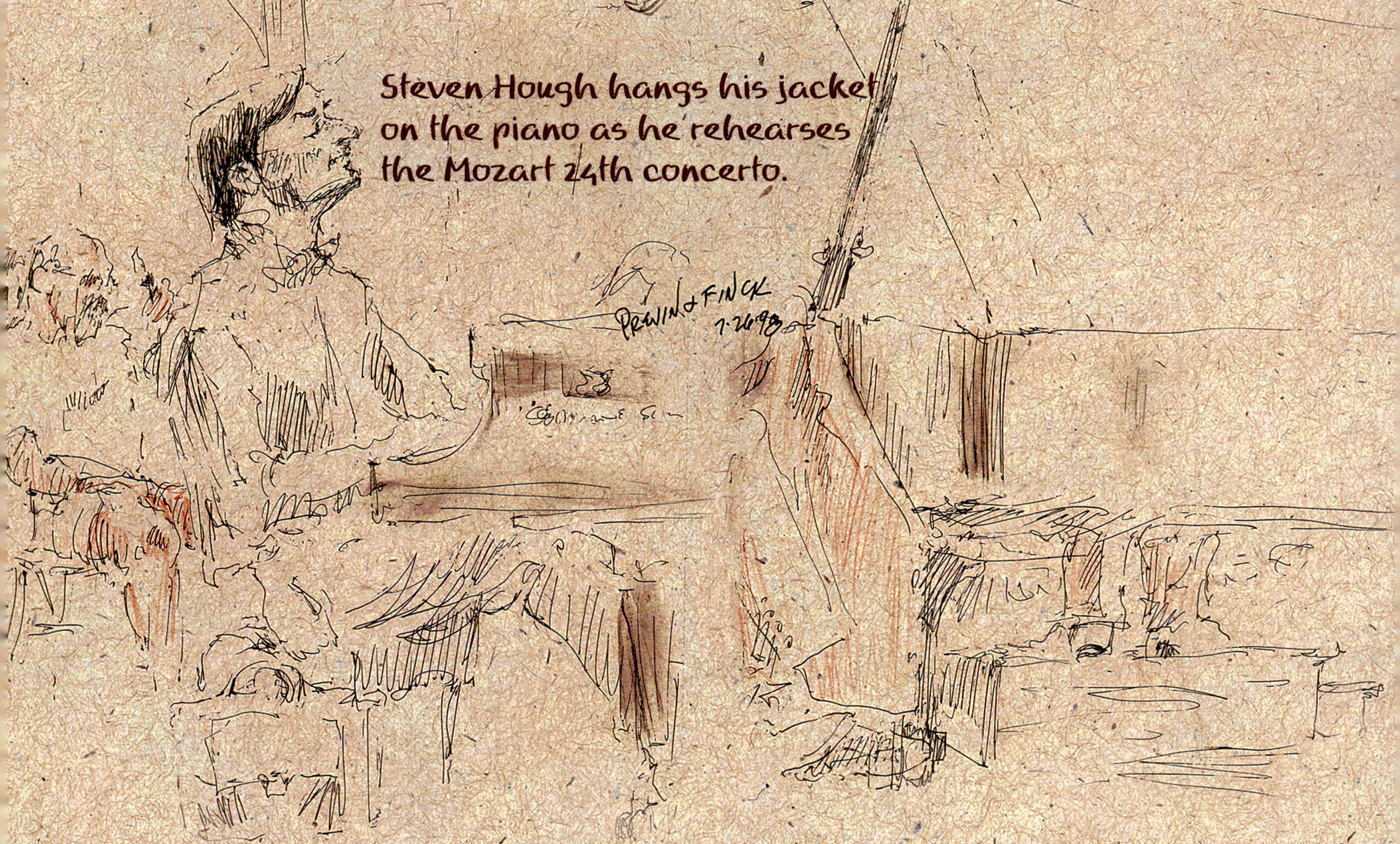

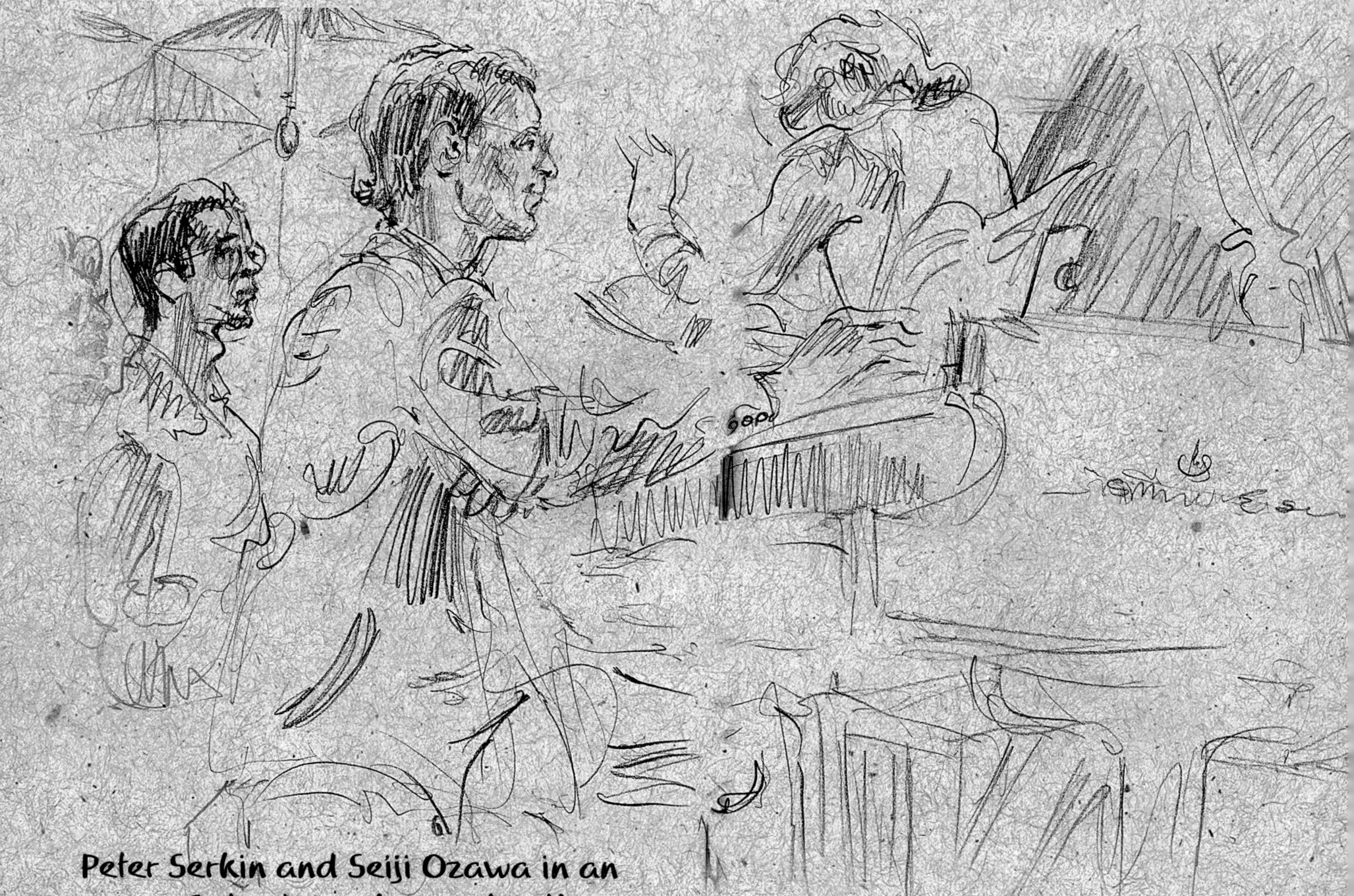

Peter Serkin and Seiji Ozawa in an open Saturday rehearsal in the Tanglewood Shed.

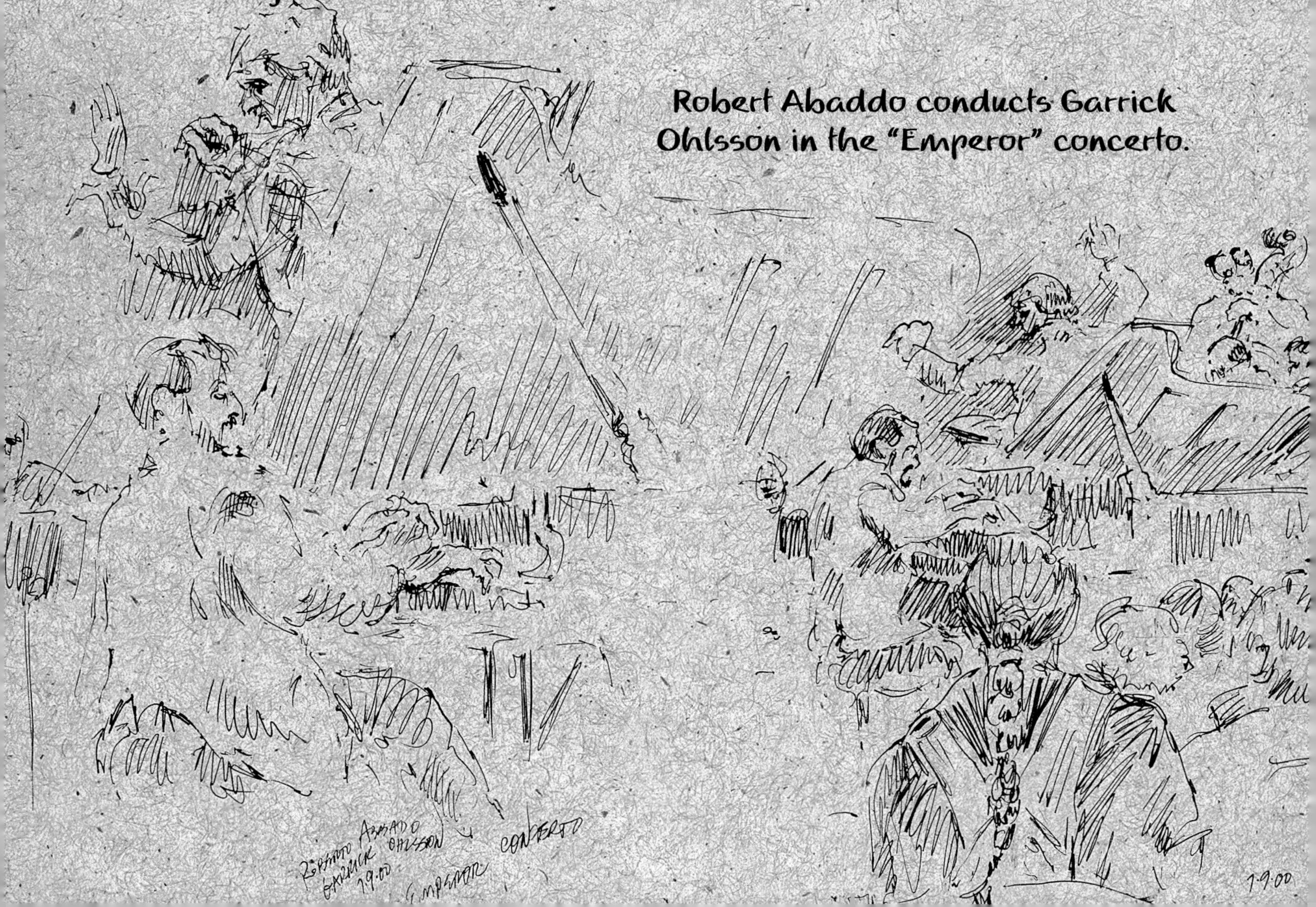

Robert Abaddo conducts Garrick Ohlsson in the "Emperor" concerto.

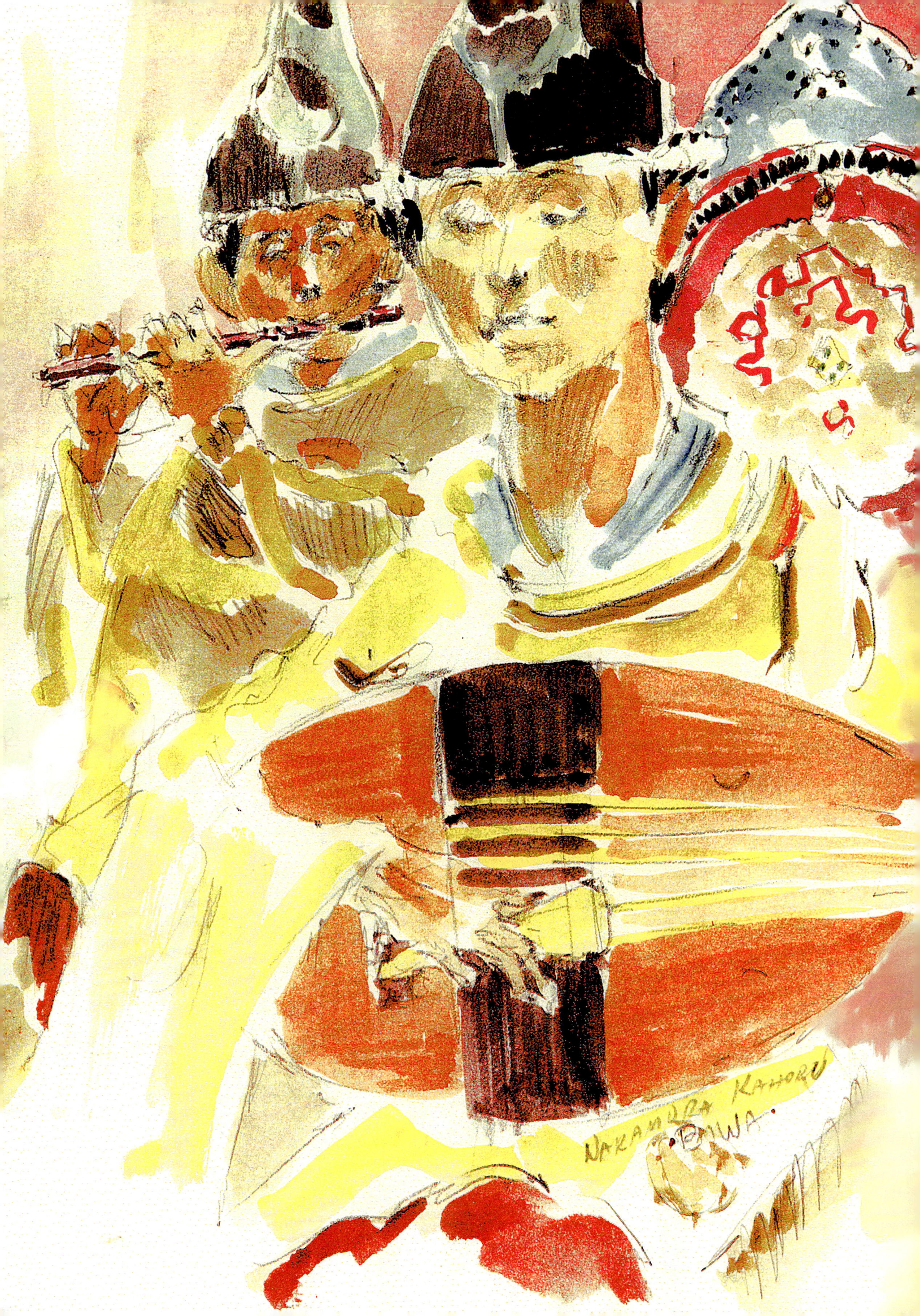
NAKAMURA KAHORU
BIWA.

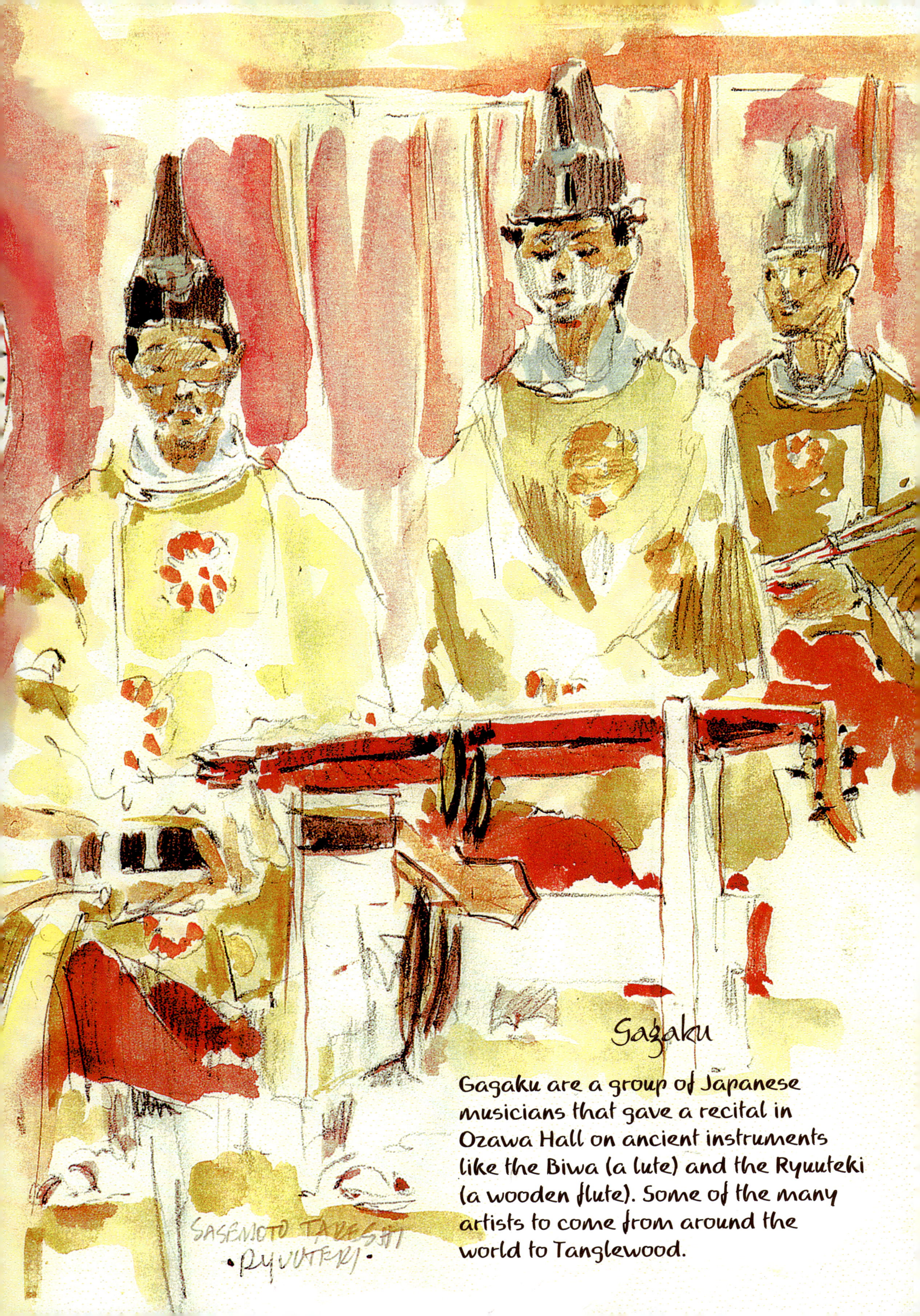

Gagaku

Gagaku are a group of Japanese musicians that gave a recital in Ozawa Hall on ancient instruments like the Biwa (a lute) and the Ryuuteki (a wooden flute). Some of the many artists to come from around the world to Tanglewood.

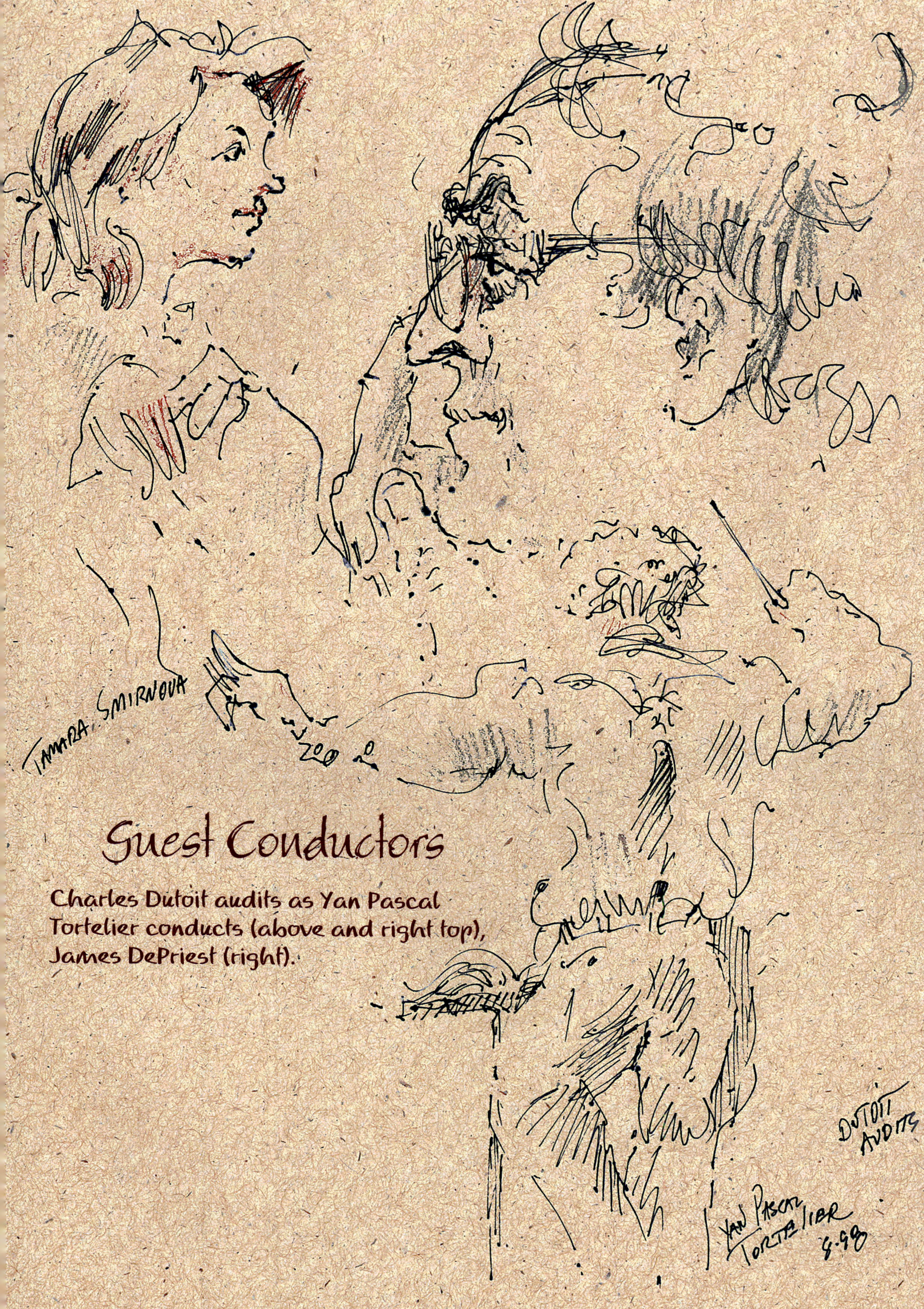

Guest Conductors

Charles Dutoit audits as Yan Pascal Tortelier conducts (above and right top), James DePriest (right).

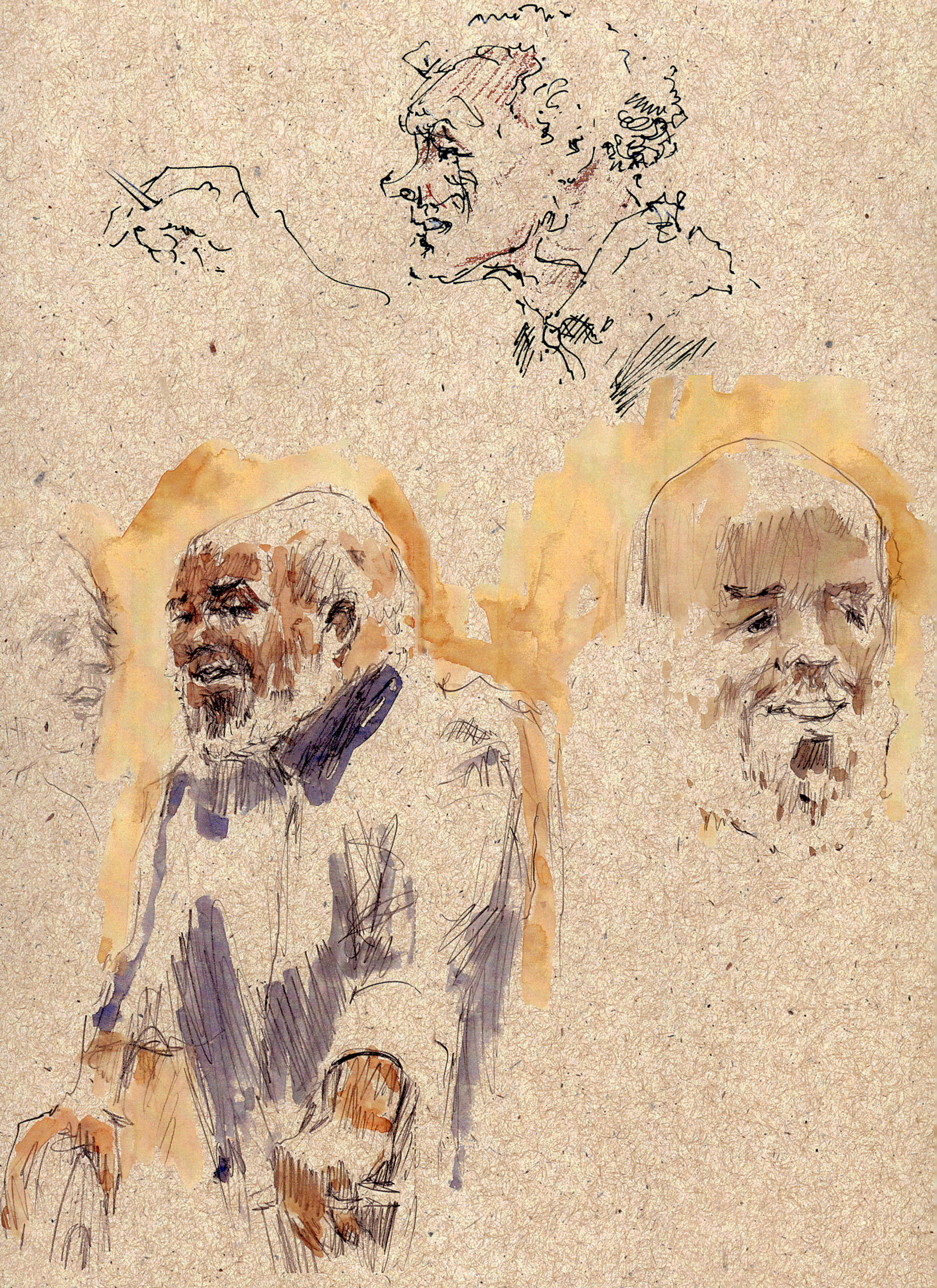

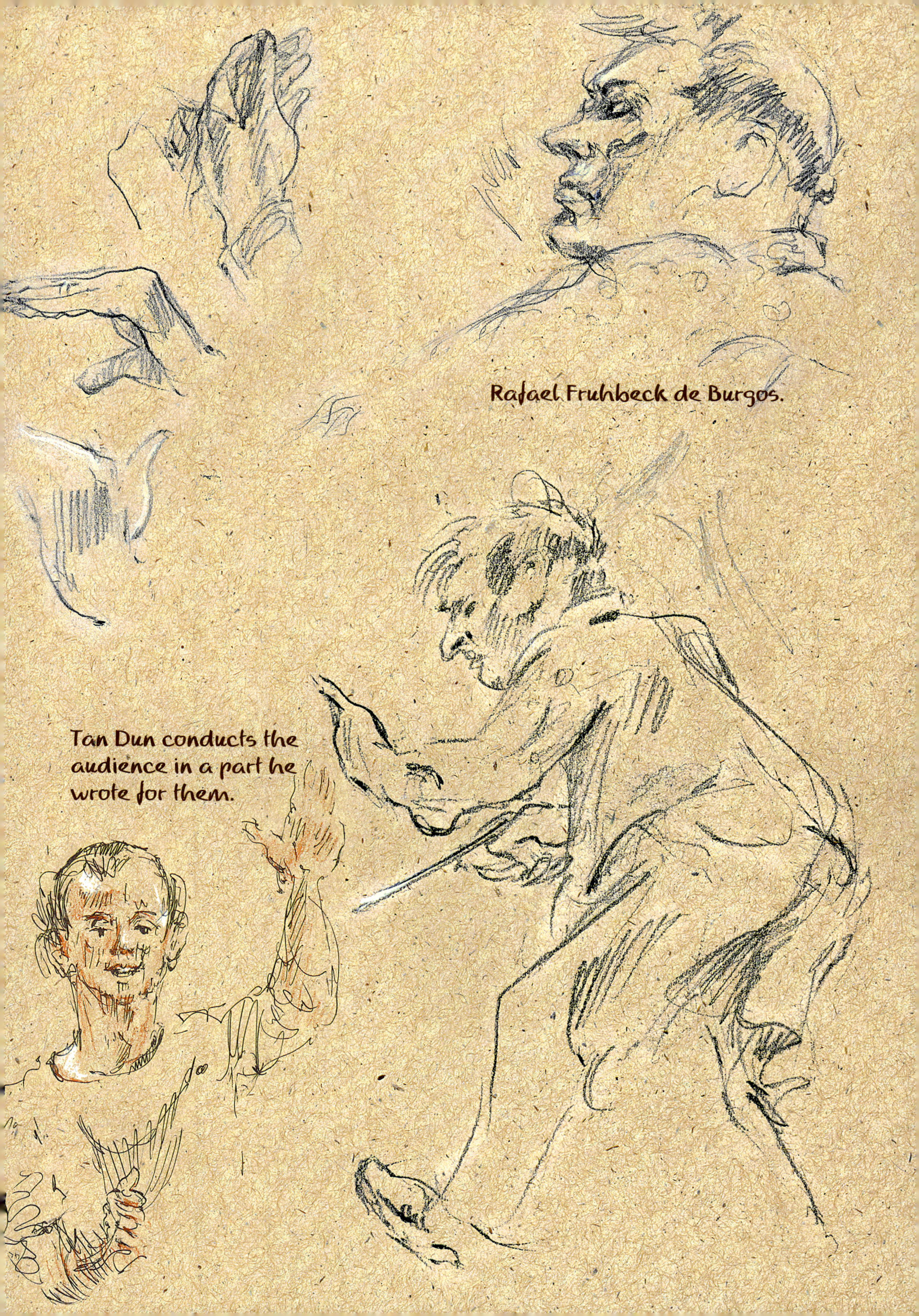
Rafael Fruhbeck de Burgos.
Tan Dun conducts the audience in a part he wrote for them.

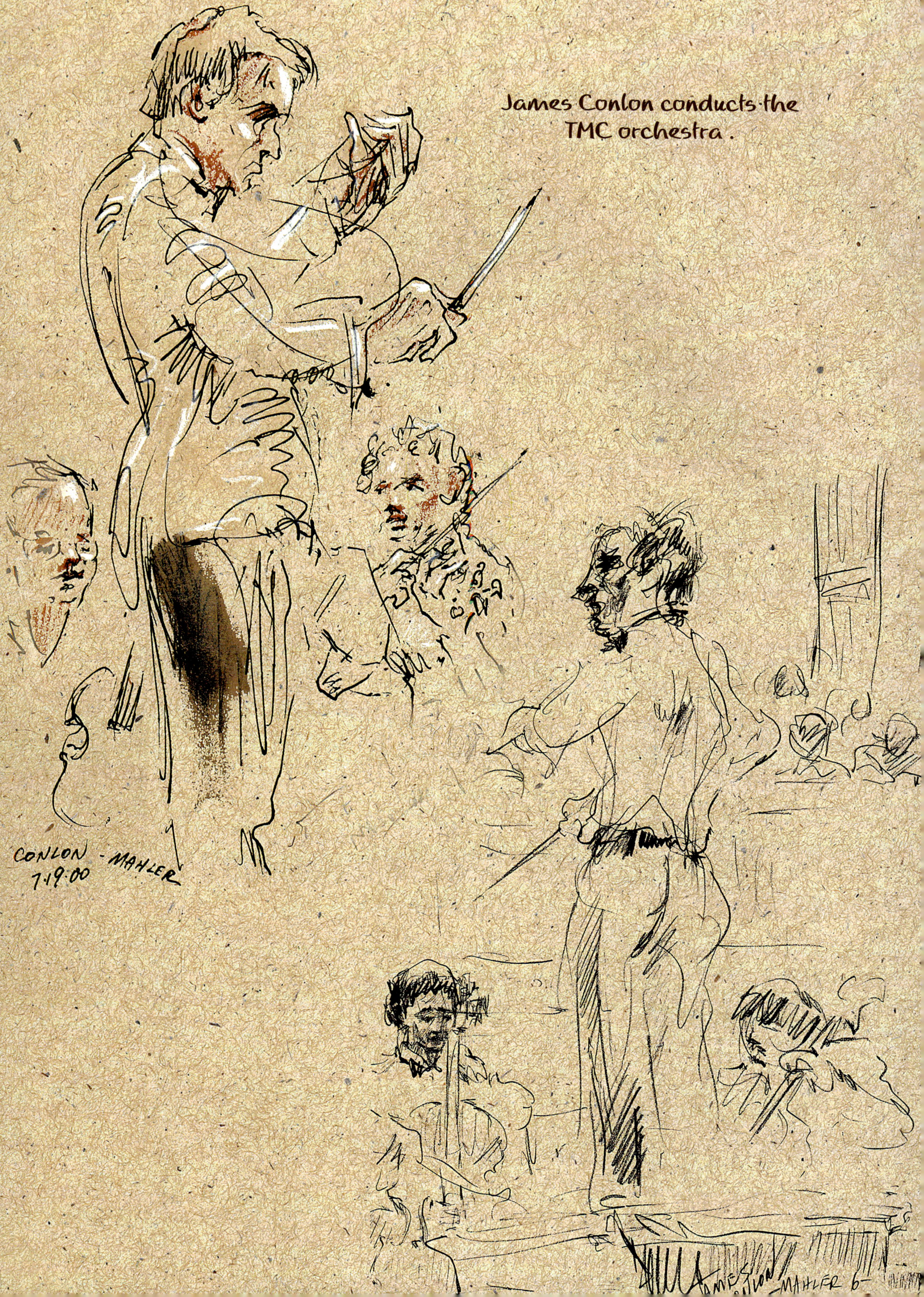

James Conlon conducts the TMC orchestra.

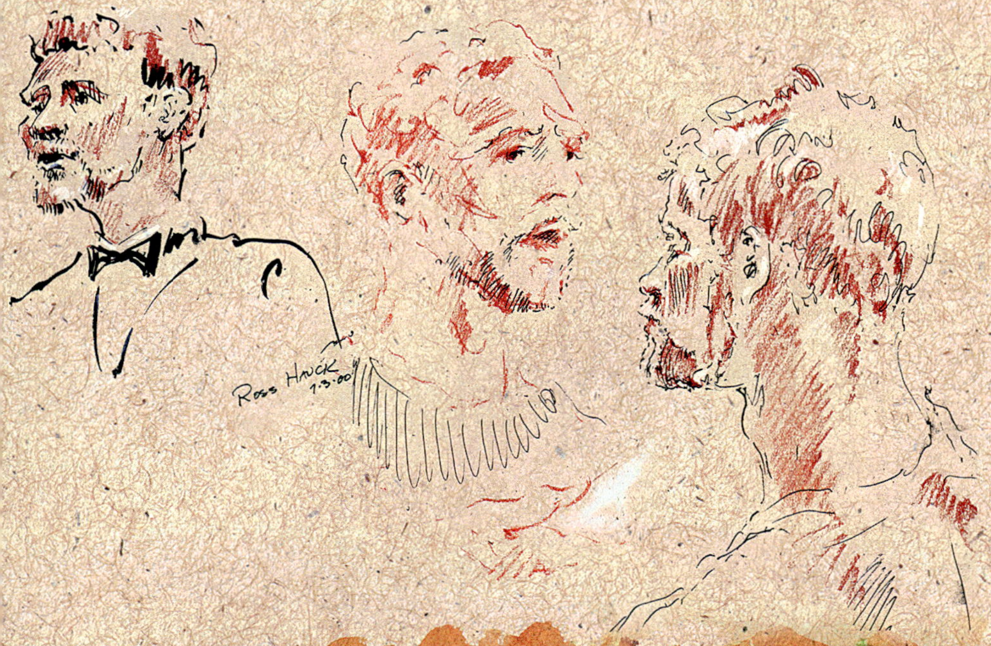

Phyllis Curtin's Master Class

This class is unique. You can sit under an oak near her studio and watch her transform red-haired Ross Hauk or Jana Batty (right) into full voice and full dress, ready for the concert stage. Pure magic!

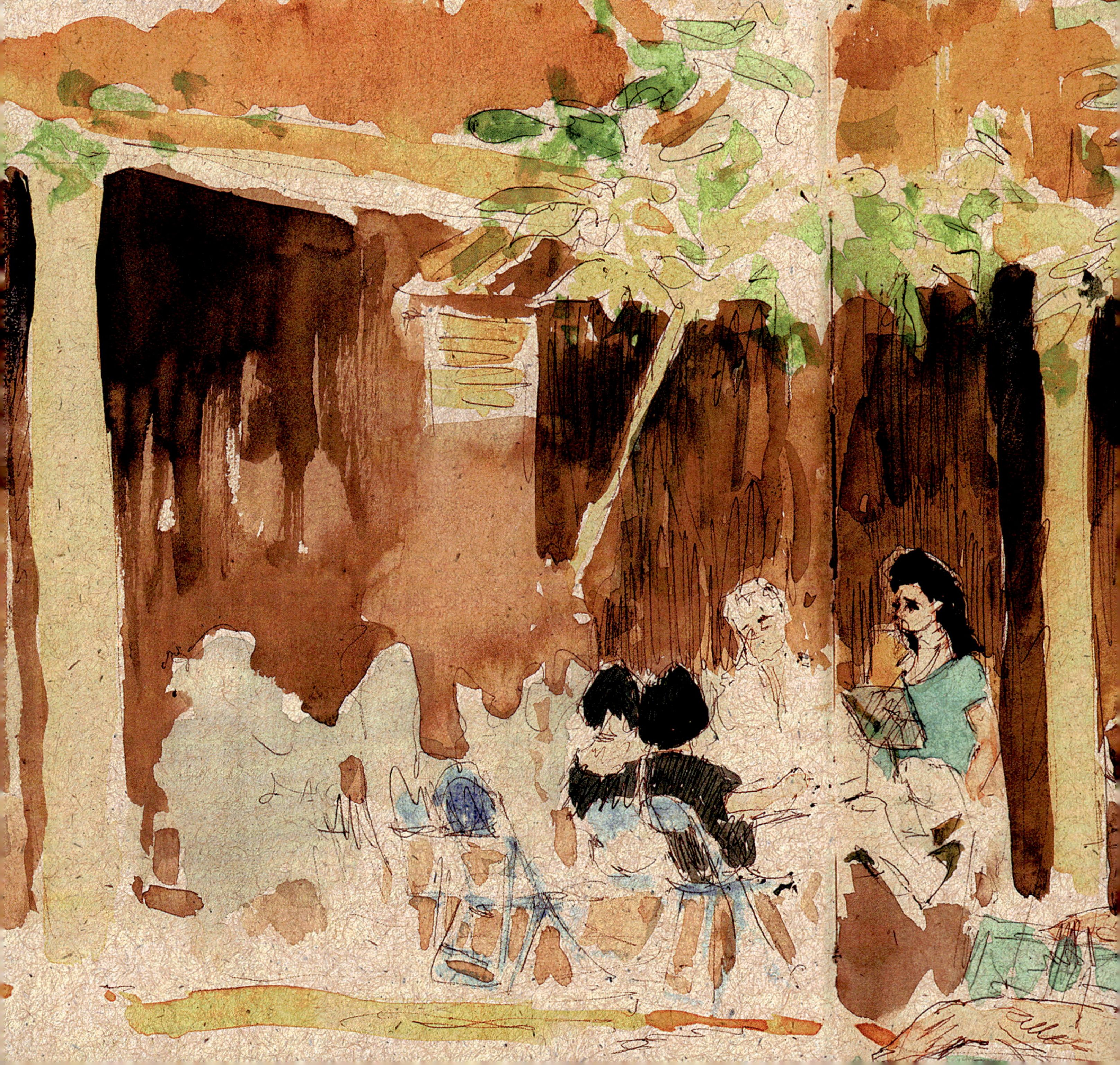

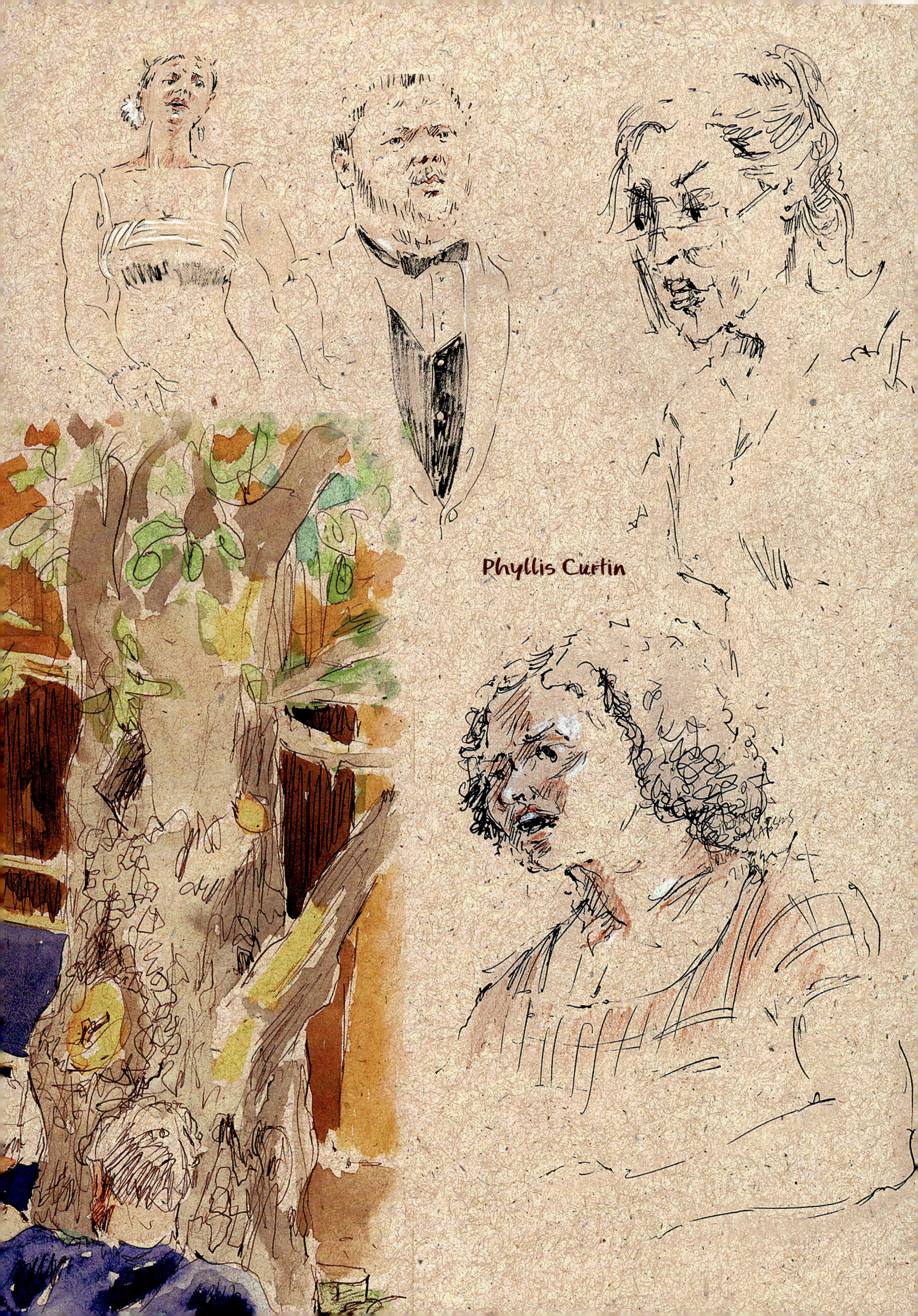
Phyllis Curtin

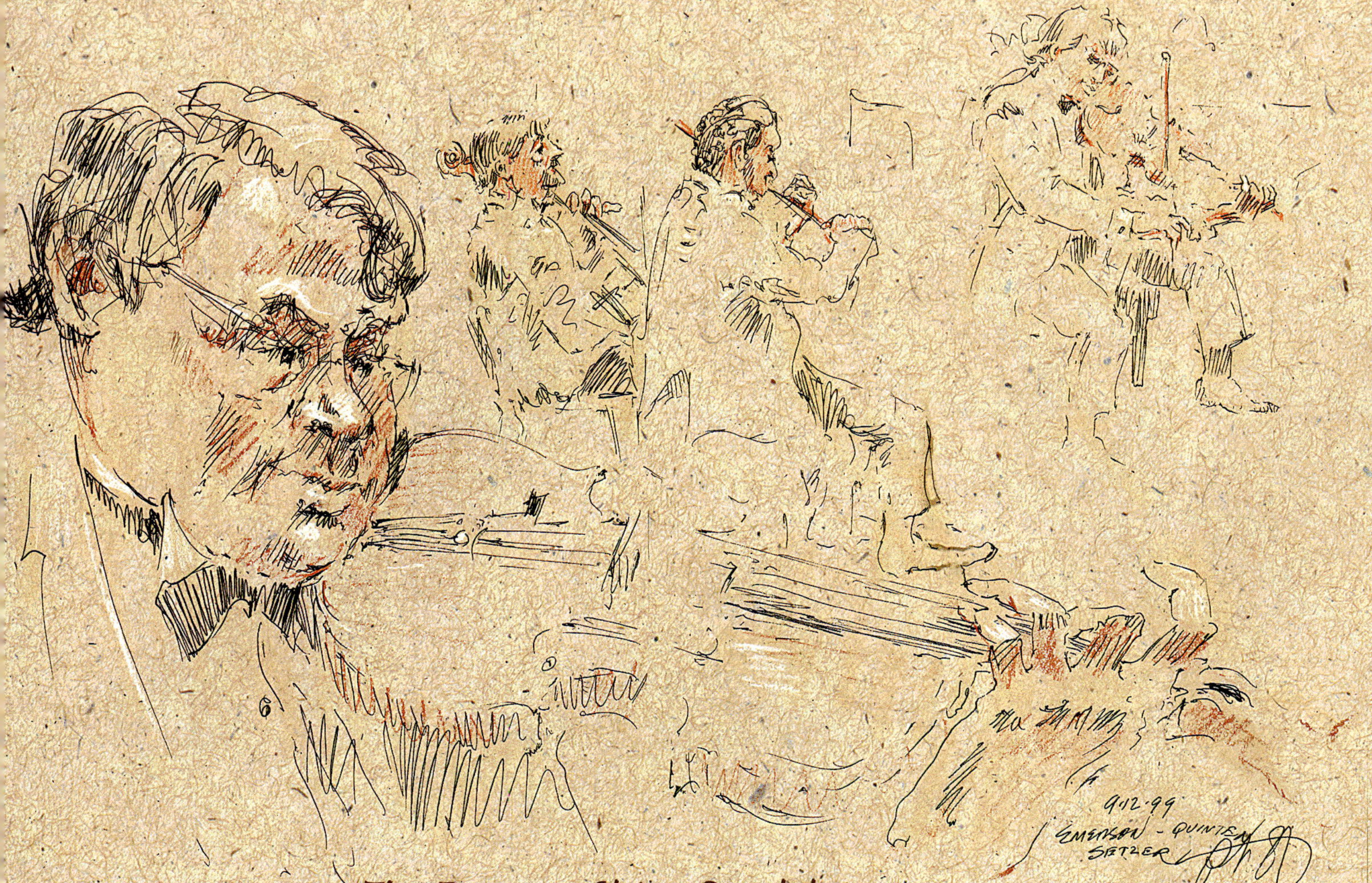

The Emerson String Quartet.

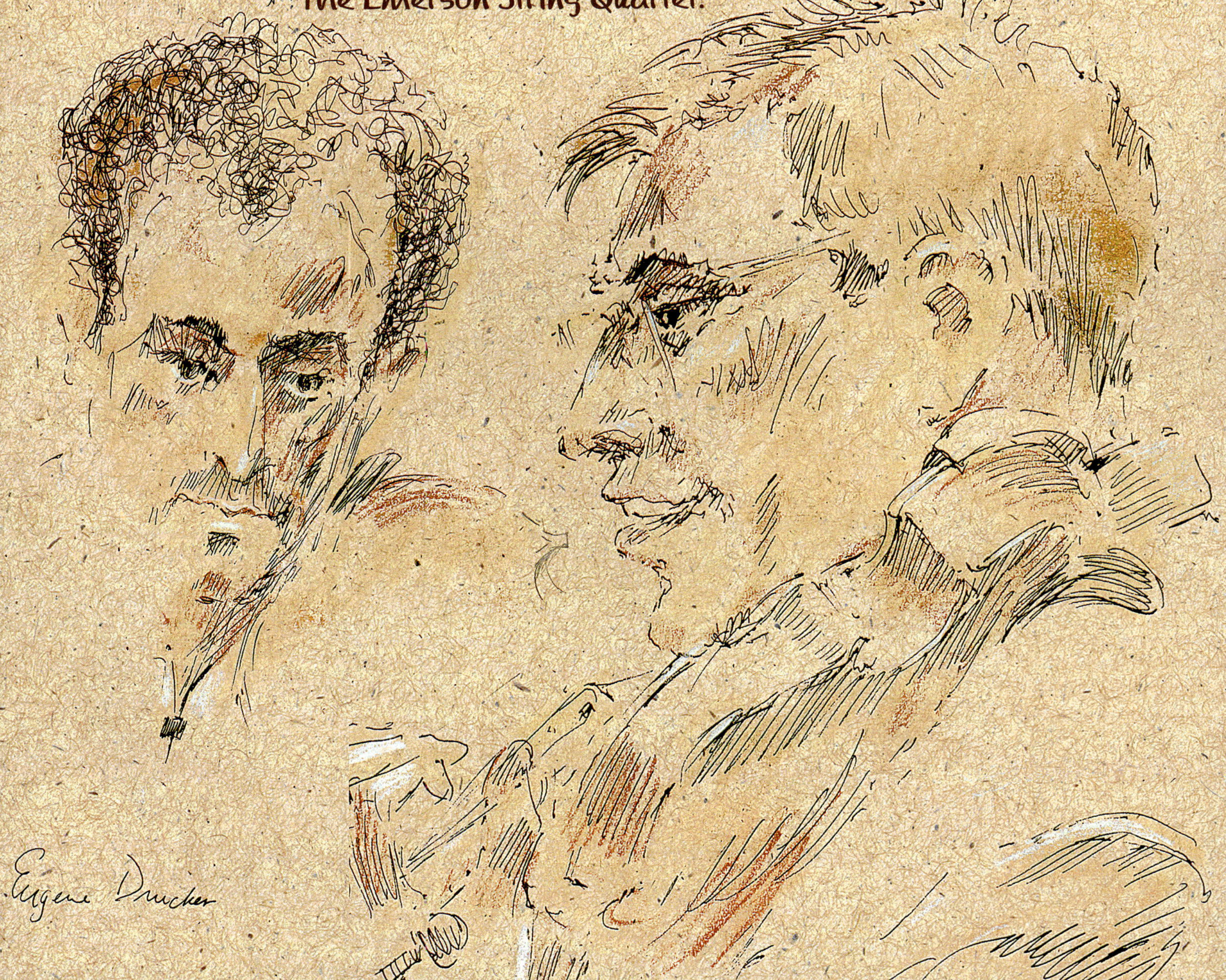

String Quartets

The Emerson Quartet, with David Finckel, cellist, Philip Setzer, first violin (top left), Eugene Drucker, first violin (they take turns) and Lawrence Dutton, viola (bottom left).

The Tokyo Quartet, with Kikue Ikeda, second violin and Michael Kopelman, first violin.

A selection from a future volume on string ensembles.

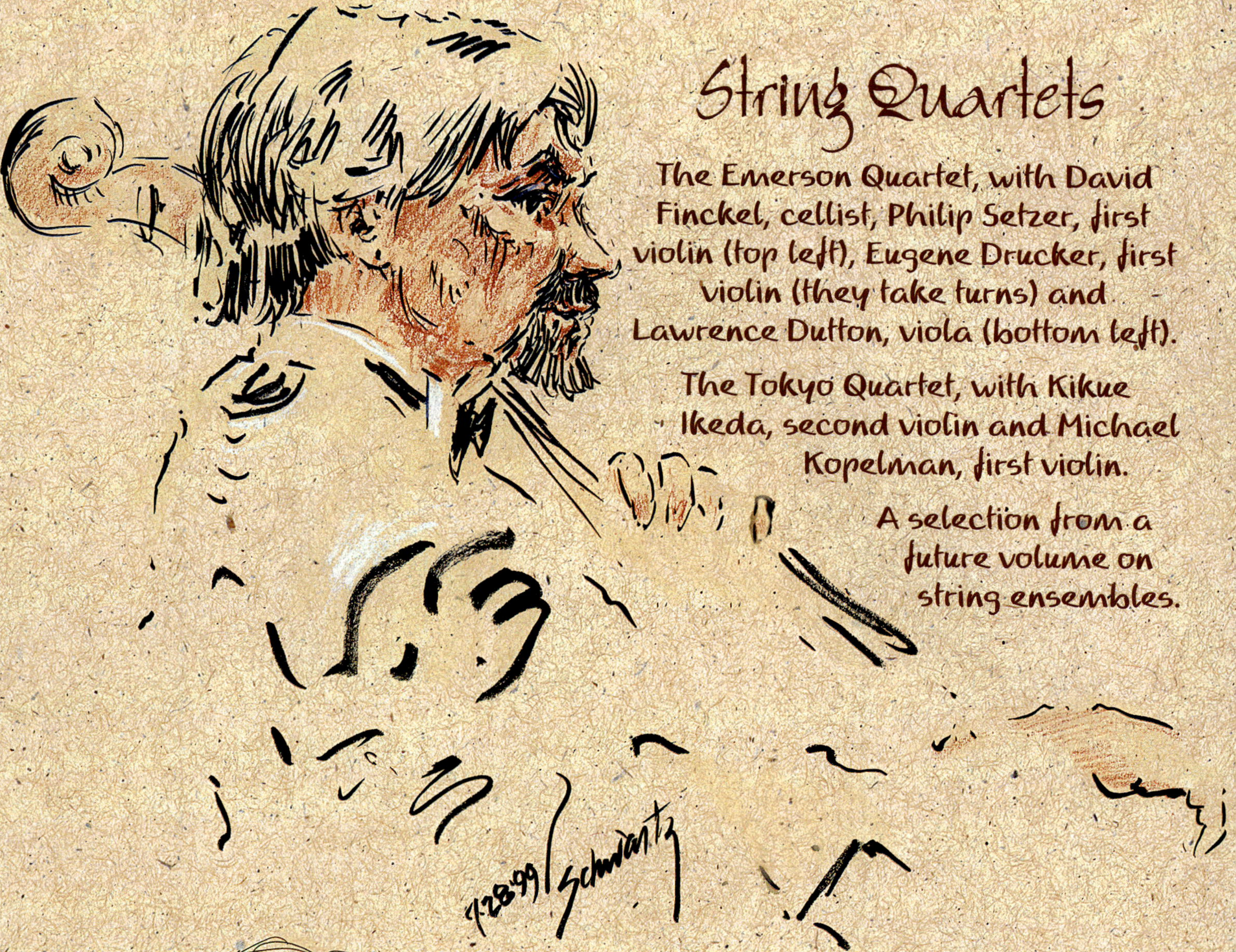

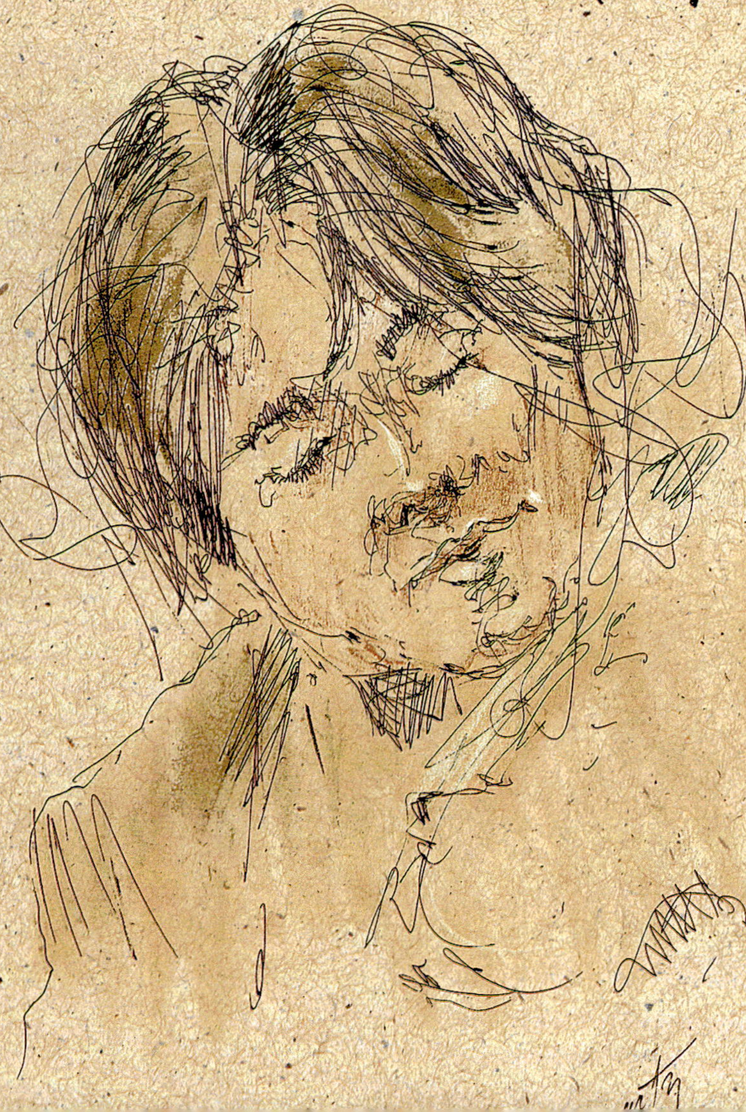

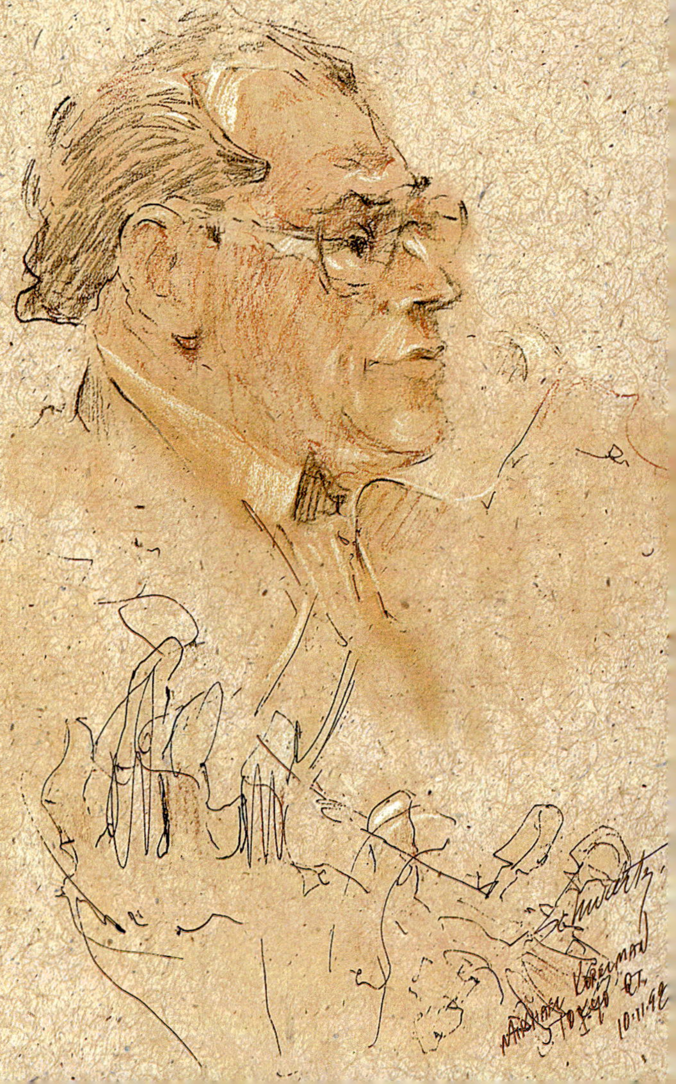

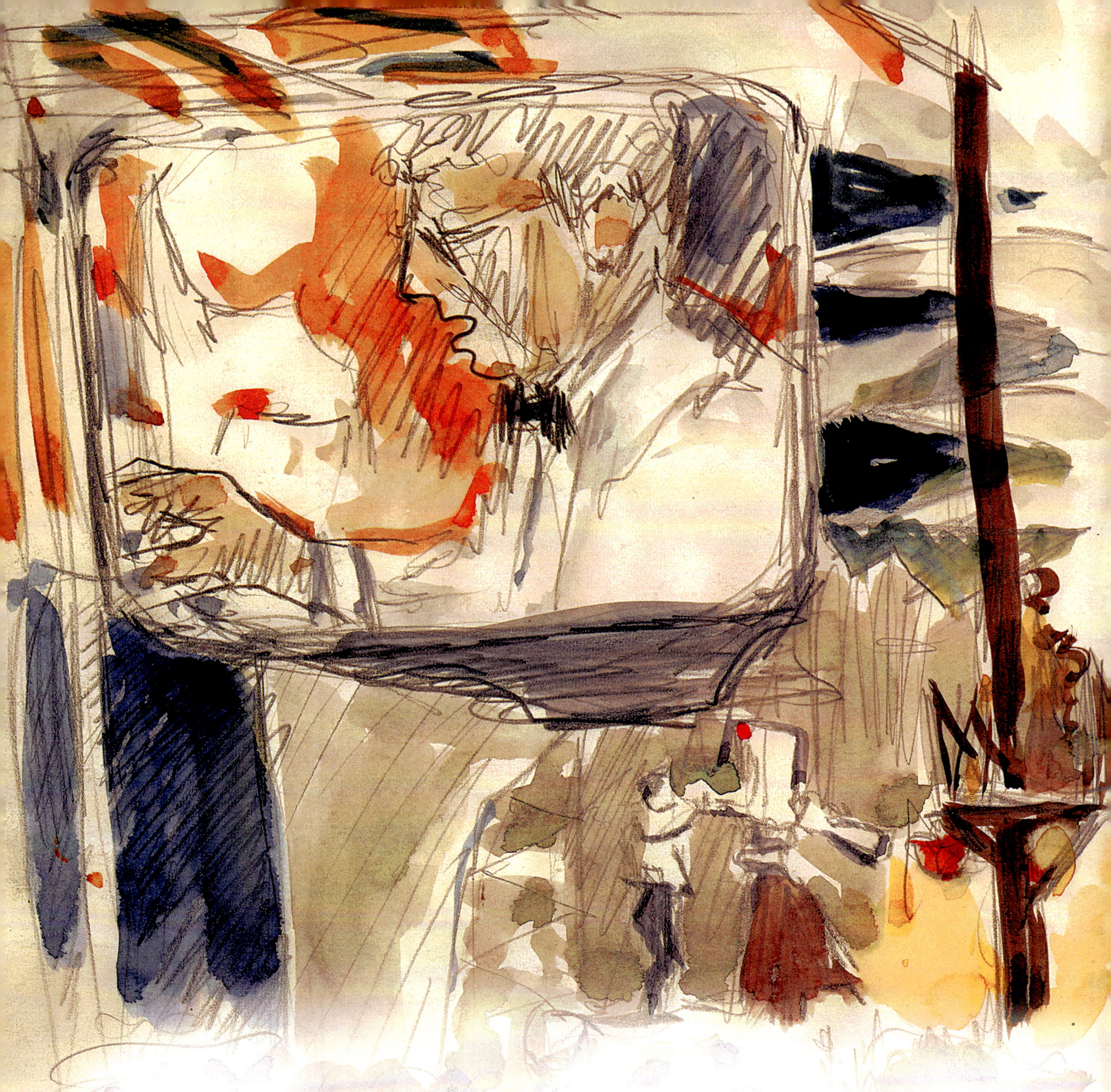

The Tanglewood Shed

On a historic night. This was the first closed circuit T.V. broadcast that allowed the audience on the lawn and at the back of the Shed to SEE as well as hear the concert, with John Browning at the piano. My vantage point was outside in back of the Shed where the orchestra seemed only a golden glow. I could barely make out the grand piano and Ozawa, but now, I could clearly see Browning at the keyboard as if I were on the stage with the cameraman.

The audience on the lawn, tried and true music lovers, the heart of Tanglewood, who brave the elements and rarely ever see the performers up close, loved it!

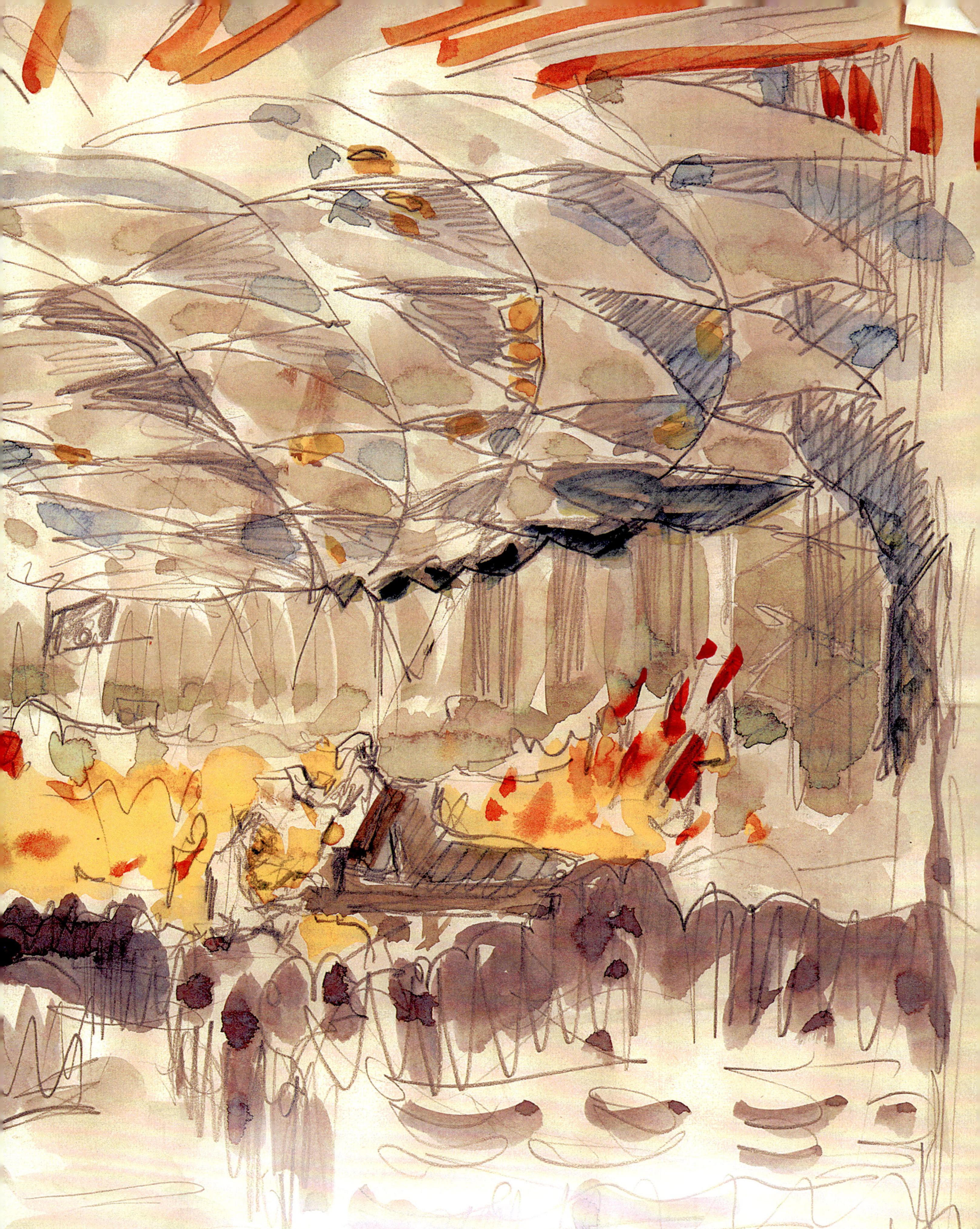

All of us come to Tanglewood because there is nothing to equal these live musical performances. I hope that some of these images can reinvoke the pleasure of some special moment for you.

The Audience

Very often I'm struck by some of the people sitting around me. Sometimes I just can't see the musicians because I don't have an advantageous seat. So, I have included a few of the many drawings I've done of the audience listening to music.

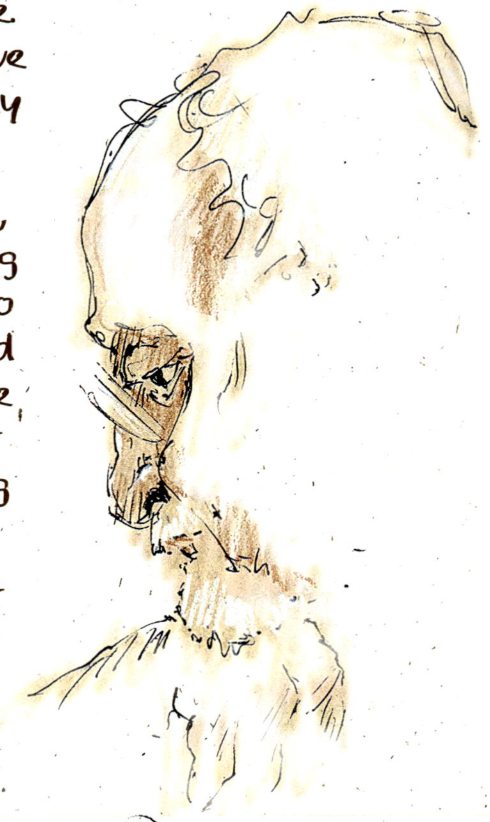

Below a beautiful young woman; a simple contour drawing, you can see her concentration and the pleasure she's getting out of the music. The second drawing is one of my wife who was a regular companion at these musical events and loved them a great deal. She could sit anywhere, even way in the back because she was just listening, whereas I have to get close to see detail. Here she is, head in hand, concentrating on the music. This book was meant for her.

If you are part of the Tanglewood audience it is also meant for you.

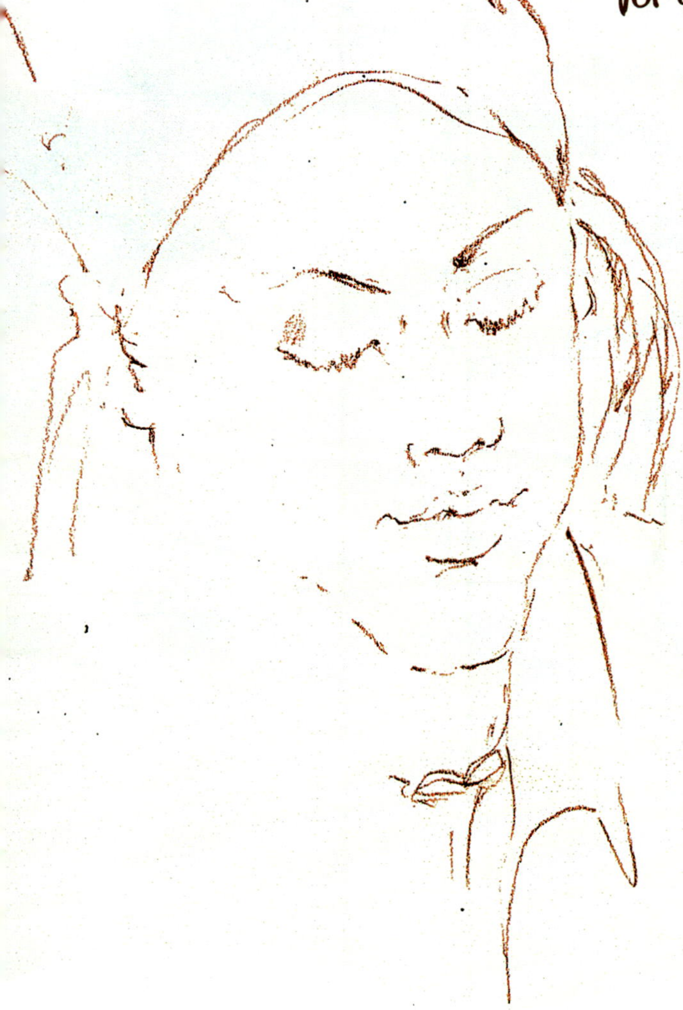

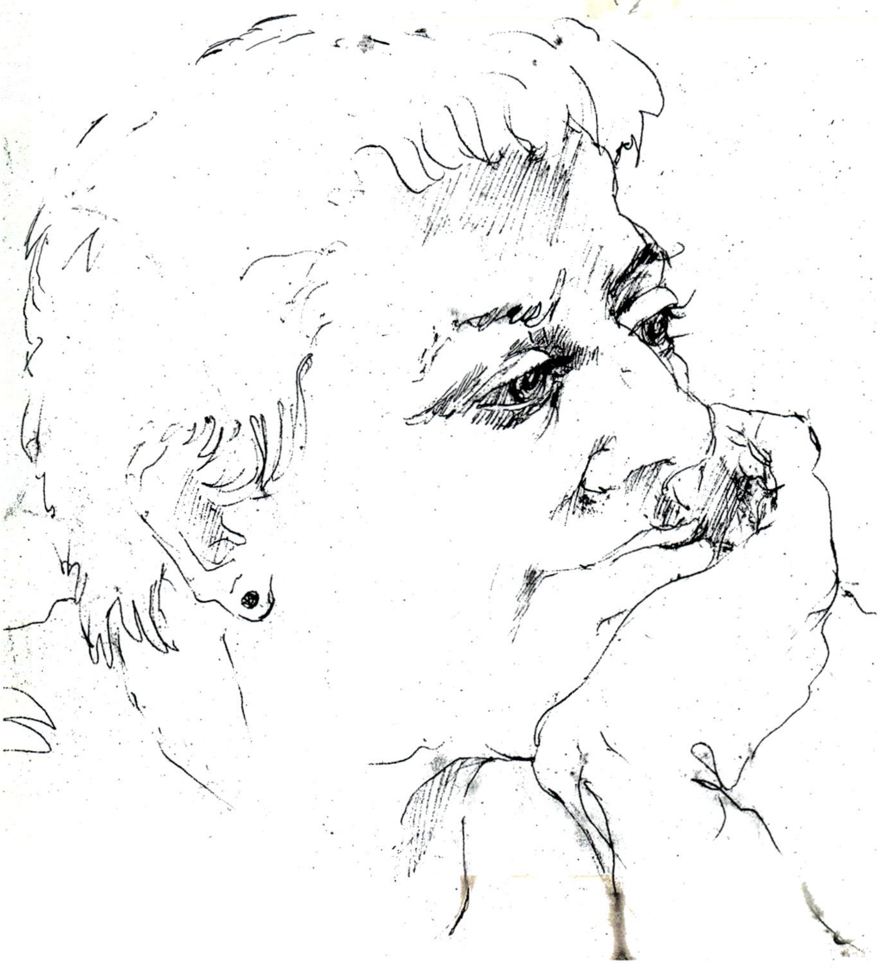